Also by Meri Wallace

Keys to Parenting Your Four Year Old

Birth Order Blues

MERI WALLACE, M.S.W.

Birth Order Blues

How Parents
Can Help Their Children
Meet the Challenges
of Birth Order

AN OWL BOOK

HENRY HOLT AND COMPANY

NEW YORK

12732335

Henry Holt and Company, Inc.
Publishers since 1866
115 West 18th Street
New York, New York 10011

Henry Holt® is a registered
trademark of Henry Holt and Company, Inc.

Library of Congress Cataloging-in-Publication Data
Wallace, Meri.
Birth order blues : how parents can help their children
meet the challenges of birth order /
Meri Wallace.—1st Owl book ed.
p.   cm.
Includes bibliographical references and index.
ISBN 0-8050-5210-0 (pbk. : alk. paper)
1. Birth order.   2. Sibling rivalry.   3. Parent and child.   I. Title.
BF723.B5W35   1999
155.9'24—dc21   98-39660

Henry Holt books are available for special promotions and
premiums. For details contact: Director, Special Markets.

First Owl Book Edition 1999

Designed by Victoria Hartman

Printed in the United States of America
All first editions are printed on acid-free paper.∞

10   9   8   7   6   5   4   3   2   1

To Jonathan,
my husband and best friend
For the unconditional love and emotional support
you give me in life, your countless pep talks, and for
editing and lending your wisdom to this book.

To my dearest son Michael
and daughter-in-law Meredith
For giving me immeasurable joy and pride as a parent
as I watch you both grow and for your continuous love
and support all the way through this endeavor.

Contents

Acknowledgments

🐝 My deepest appreciation to Nina Calaman, my administrator and my friend, who has given her heart and soul to this project. Her exceptional computer skills, her endless hard work and devotion, and her constant emotional support have all helped make this book possible.

I am most grateful to Wendy Sherman, the publisher of Owl Books, and my editor, Cynthia Vartan, for their commitment to this project and for giving me the opportunity to write this book. Cynthia's expert guidance and the respect, warmth, and constant support that she offered me made this a very pleasurable experience. I am indebted to Bruce Ostler and my literary agent, Ivy Fischer Stone, for believing in my book and helping me to launch it.

I have been very fortunate to be associated with Ira Wolfman, editorial director, and Susan Lapinski, editor, at *Sesame Street Parents*, who have given me the wonderful opportunity to write a column in the magazine.

I wish to acknowledge Lydia Weaver, my first editor, who gave me confidence as a writer and taught me the tools of the trade; Luciano Rammairone and Gina Bianciardi for giving me the opportunity to write a column for *Brooklyn Parent Magazine* for the past four years; and Betsy Wolfe, for granting me a monthly column in *New York Family* magazine for several years.

My deepest gratitude to Richard Cohen, M.S.W., B.C.D., Dr. Jeff Seinfeld, and Laura Benedik, M.S.W., C.S.W., for nurturing my career as a therapist and teaching me the most about how to listen to people, to hear what they are really saying, and to respond in a helpful, sensitive way; and to Karen Cwalinski, M.S.W., C.S.W., my dear friend, for reading my manuscript.

I am forever grateful to Amy Silverman, Garnett Falzetta, Cindy Harden, Patti Schackett, Rachel Reyser, Stefanie Shabman, and Teri Fabi who have so graciously taken time away from their busy schedules to talk to me about their children and have been of immeasurable help to me in writing this book. My sincerest thanks to the staffs of York Avenue Preschool and Open House Nursery School for their constant support with my writing projects and for being such exemplary educators to work with and learn from.

All my deepest appreciation to the members of my family and my friends for supporting my work and understanding all the times I have been unavailable.

My mother, Niravi Payne, has been a constant support of my professional and personal growth and a vibrant, successful role model for me. I am so proud of her recently published book, *The Whole Person Fertility Program*. My father, Albert Libuser, has always been a source of love, companionship, and strength for me, and my stepmother, Arlene Libuser, embraced me as a daughter early on in our relationship, and has always been there for me and my family. My special thanks to my sister Bonnee, for all the fun, creative times we shared together as children and the support and guidance she has given me in my life. It is with deep love and affection that I thank my nephews David and Gregg, their wives Debbie and Lori, and their children, Ashley, Landon, Steven, Tyler, and Megan, and Heather Saffran, for being such constant sources of joy and support in my life.

I am especially grateful to all the wonderful adults and children that I have ever worked with as a therapist and a support group leader. They have been my best teachers and have helped me to grow professionally and personally. I would also like to express my deepest appreciation to all those individuals who participated in the interviews for this project. Though they are far too numerous to mention, each and every one has contributed to the rich anecdotes and insights in this book.

Preface

I was driving home after interviewing a charming eleven-year-old boy for this book, and was feeling very upset for him. He was hurting and I wanted to help him. But what he was experiencing was not so different from any firstborn child whom I had ever met or listened to. His tale reinforced that what I was writing about—the impact that birth order has upon a child's emotional experience—was true, and that what I had to say to parents was crucial. I had heard similar complaints before: "I have to stack the dishwasher and throw out the garbage all the time, while my two brothers run off to play." "When Mom is busy, I always have to take them along to my friend's house." "I can't keep those two out of my room. They're always messing up my things." And the list goes on. These seemingly benign issues affected his daily life, often making him feel resentful, ill-treated, less loved than his siblings, and very much alone.

But his well-meaning parents often had no clue about how hard all this was for him. Like many parents, they were unaware that children can feel so upset about these issues and that their own behavior was adding to the problems, or they were just too busy trying to get through the day that they did not notice. Every time he tried to communicate his feelings to them, they were either too distracted to listen, too pained by the information, or so offended by his delivery that he was deemed as having an attitude (which he probably did, at times), and he ended up ignored, yelled at, or punished. In return, he either battled his parents hard, or bottled up his emotions and withdrew. And so life continued for him on a daily basis, with an underlying dull ache.

This young boy needed to understand that many children in his birth order position have the same kinds of feelings, so he would know that his jealousy and resentment were normal and acceptable. He also needed his parents to make changes: some simple, such as including all the children in cleanup; some more time-consuming, such as spending time alone with him so that he would feel special; and some more profound, requiring a change in their style of communicating with him. His parents needed to sit down with him and talk about what was troubling him, rather than just reacting to his behavior. Furthermore, they needed to work with him more sensitively on these birth order issues. But the situation was certainly fixable, and these changes would make a huge difference in the way he felt about himself and his family.

From listening to youngest and middle siblings over the years as a therapist, I knew that there were common trends in their emotional experiences, too. Along with the advantages that they experienced in their positions, which I will talk about extensively in this book, like the firstborn child, they also faced some particular challenges. They too greatly needed assistance from and better communication with their parents.

As I listened to parents talk about their family problems, I saw that these birth order issues were often at the bottom of many sibling battles commonly labeled as sibling rivalry and that they often created havoc in the parent-child relationship. A parent's ongoing screaming battles with an uncooperative firstborn child, who was angry because she felt more was expected of her than her younger siblings, caused deep suffering on everyone's part. Furthermore, sometimes this friction became the cornerstone of their relationship for life.

Birth order issues also caused more subtle problems in families, such as a secondborn's tendency to underachieve because his older sister was a star pupil. They turned family life upside down and left parents feeling upset and defeated. Not only did I see these problems actively affecting children in their family life, but it was apparent to me that they followed children as they grew. As a consultant to nursery schools, I observed these difficulties being played out in the classroom, whether it was a firstborn child insisting upon being first or a secondborn child pushing around another child to make up for being dominated at home. In my clinical practice, I spotted these issues causing problems for adults in their workplace, marriages, and family relationships. Zeroing in on these early childhood emotional experiences and resolving them as early as possible proved to be of significant help to people in all these situations.

The first time that I remember actually crystallizing my ideas about the birth order experience was when I was preparing a workshop on sibling rivalry for a woman's center. In preparation, I wrote out an outline—oldest, middle, youngest child—and described the particular struggles of each. It felt so right. After all, each child's issues were different. My presentation was organized according to this format, and I even used the outline as a handout. The mothers at the workshop strongly related to what I was saying. They found that it was beneficial to view a family situation from each child's particular slant and talk about ways to work with each child in the birth order.

Over the years, I have presented my ideas to parents in therapy, in support groups, and in workshops, and time and time again, parents have found them immeasurably helpful. Their children were doing better and they felt more competent as parents. Best of all, their family lives improved.

In this book, I show you the powerful effect that birth order has upon the way children see themselves, their relationships with their parents and siblings, and their development. I describe what daily life is like for each child in his or her birth order position and point out both the positives of the experience and some of the emotional difficulties each faces. As we go along, I give suggestions on how to talk to your children about these issues and what strategies to use that will help you to be more emotionally present for each of your children.

The material I present to you has evolved from my seventeen years of professional experience as a therapist and parent support group and workshop leader, and from direct interviews with adults and children of all ages. Though I have done much formal research for this project, I have found that listening to people is my best resource. To safeguard the privacy of all the individuals who have contributed to this work, I have either used fictitious names, altered the details, or created characters who are a composite of many different people. However, the potency of their stories prevails.

I hope that the insights and tools I offer you will give you greater confidence as a parent, bring you closer to your child, and help you and your child to have a more enjoyable relationship.

Birth Order Blues

The
Birth Order
Experience

"My three-year-old son, Sam, is going crazy," a distraught mother announced at one of our evening parent support group meetings. Her extreme anxiety permeated the air, and the mothers and I drew in close to listen to her and to help.

Slowly, she began to unveil what was causing her to feel so worried. Her son had suddenly changed from an angelic, complaisant child into an aggressive one. She gave an example: The night before, she had come home and found her son tearing all of her daughter's drawings off the wall in a frenzy. What had caused such a reaction? We began to dig a little deeper beneath the surface and tried to piece together what had happened.

Apparently, Sam had been building an airplane out of the couch cushions. Five-year-old Elizabeth had plunked herself down on one of them, and when he asked her to move, she refused. No amount of pleading or tugging at her could get her to budge. Finally, feeling exasperated, he ran into her room and started yanking her works of art off the wall. Then she moved.

As we talked, it became clear that this pattern of interaction between the two children was becoming a daily occurrence. Gradually, I helped this mother see that her son's behavior, which she thought was so bizarre, had to do with his being the younger child in the family. He was acting this way because he was upset. In fact, what was happening with Sam naturally occurred in families. For three years his older sister had dominated him, and because she was so much stronger, he often felt helpless to fight back. Now, at a stage in his development when he was feeling a greater sense of self, he was trying to stand up to her. Sam needed help in understanding what his struggle as a younger sibling was all about, and in finding more positive ways to deal with his emotions. He needed a great deal of emotional support, too.

Not only was Sam graphically demonstrating his struggle as a younger sibling, but Elizabeth was revealing her problems as an older sibling. Elizabeth had viewed Sam as an intrusion in her life for three years, ever since he moved into her space by being born. And she was upset, too. Now, Elizabeth was encroaching on his space as a way of getting back at him. Just as being the center of her parents' attention was taken away from her, she would take away something from her younger brother. Like Sam, Elizabeth also needed support and help in understanding her feelings and behavior related to her birth order position. She, too, must learn more appropriate ways of expressing herself.

Once we talked through the issues in the group, Elizabeth and Sam's mother relaxed. Her son was not crazy. She could do something; she would go home and try out our suggestions. As a matter of fact, she did and things got better.

But Sam and Elizabeth and their parents are not alone. When you scratch beneath the surface of many children's behaviors, you will find birth order issues, or problems related to their position in the family, as the source. For example, why isn't Jennifer able to succeed in math? Perhaps it is because her older brother is a math genius. Why does Jason fight his parents over every request they make? Maybe, because he is the oldest child, his parents ask him to do more than his younger sister. Why is middleborn Peter always acting like a clown? He might be acting this way because he feels his older and younger siblings are getting more attention than he is and negative attention seems better than none.

By a twist of fate, a child is born into a particular position in the family, and from this place, she will attempt to share her parents' love and attention and get her basic emotional and physical needs met. This setup naturally causes jealousies and resentment among siblings. However, as each child interacts with his parents and siblings, there will be some common characteristics in the positive and negative emotional experiences she will have, determined by her special spot in the family. These are all part of a child's birth order experience.

There is no doubt that there are certain advantages to each child's position in the family. The firstborn gets to stay up latest, the middle child has an older sibling to rely on and a younger sibling to look up to her, and the youngest gets to be the baby. It is true, too, that having a sibling can be a very pleasurable and positive experience for children. In fact, it is through this relationship that children receive their first lessons about how to love a peer, how to share, and how to empathize with others—skills that are then transferred to the world at large. However, what is essential to understand is that there are also some very difficult emotional challenges that children experience related to their birth order positions. These difficulties, such as being dethroned by a new baby, or feeling incompetent in relation to an older sibling, I will refer to as a child's birth order issues.

Some of the difficulties that the child encounters are related to the way he views himself, merely because of his birth order position. For example, a secondborn child may conclude, "I'm no good," because his older sister can write but he cannot. At other times, a child's unhappy feelings may be related to the way a parent responds to her in her particular position. For example, a parent may come down too hard upon a firstborn child, or fail to acknowledge a secondborn. A child's upset may also have to do with the way his siblings relate to him, such as the kind of domination the youngest child experiences because of the sibling power structure. The way the parent handles (or mishandles) the sibling relationship, such as showing favoritism to one child or endlessly comparing the two, can create problems for a child, as well. Such parental behaviors can cause a child to view herself negatively and even determine how one sibling treats another. If the parent always sides with the youngest, for example, the older siblings may be angered and vent their rage on him.

These experiences can definitely affect the child's self-esteem, her sense of well-being, and her behavior. As the child grows, any unresolved jealousy, anger, insecurity, or resentment resulting from these early childhood experiences will shape her development, and be played out at school, at work, and in her adult relationships. By taking the steps that I describe in the chapters ahead, you will learn how to help your children to feel better in their daily lives, build more positive family relationships, and prevent some future problems.

Our culture is not unfamiliar with the birth order experience. In the Bible, Cain, who was a firstborn son, was so jealous because his younger brother Abel was the preferred child that he actually killed him. Joseph's older brothers were so tormented by the fact that their father, Jacob, gave their youngest brother the famous coat of many colors and generally seemed to favor him that they planned to kill him; instead, they later ended up selling him into slavery. In Shakespearean plays, much intrigue and drama centers around the attempt of jealous younger brothers to wrench the crown away from their oldest brother who is the designated heir. Medieval laws of primogeniture, whereby the firstborn son inherited all the family lands, led to much suffering on the part of laterborns and strife among brethren.

Even very respected theorists have recognized the importance of the birth order experience in people's lives. According to Sigmund Freud, "the position of a child in the family order is a factor of extreme importance in determining the shape of his later life . . ." Alfred Adler, an early follower of Freud who later founded his own school of "individual psychology," took special interest in birth order and its effect upon children in their families. Murray Bowen, one of the originators of family systems therapy, stated, "No single piece of data is more important than knowing the sibling position of people in the present and past generations."

This book does not set out to prove that birth order is the only shaping factor in a child's life. As a traditional psychotherapist, I certainly spend a great deal of time with patients focusing on how their early parent-child relationships (unrelated to having a sibling) or particular family events have affected their lives. Nor does this book set out to show definitive character traits resulting from an individual's birth order position. I do not believe that there are definitive outcomes—a firstborn child who is pushed to succeed, as firstborns often are, can become a high achiever or can cave in under the pressure. Unfortunately, many theorists have placed too much emphasis on this aspect of birth order—so much so, that developmental experts who fear pigeonholing children (and rightly so) completely minimize the effect of birth order on experience or disavow it altogether. I believe that this is unfortunate. As we will clearly see, acknowledging that birth order does affect children and learning how is extremely important to a family's well-being.

What this book does undertake is to show you that birth order is, in fact, one major aspect of a child's experience that has a powerful impact upon his emotions and his development. Though every child's experience is somewhat different, the following are some of the most common early childhood experiences of each child in the birth order.

The firstborn child basks in her parents' undivided love and attention for a period of time and often benefits emotionally and intellectually from this experience. She can emerge with a sense of security and self-confidence. However, she also faces some difficult emotional challenges. Her inexperienced, anxious parents often have very high expectations of her, and she can end up feeling very pressured to succeed. She experiences tremendous feelings of loss as she gives up her crib and must share her parents' love for the first time when her younger sibling is born. The firstborn child feels jealous because of the special care and attention her adorable little sibling gets; feels intruded upon, because the younger one tends to mess up whatever she is doing; and is resentful because she is generally expected to behave better and to do more. She may experience a great deal of anger, but since she has been warned not to hurt her younger sibling, she may feel frightened of her emotions and have a hard time managing them.

The secondborn child benefits from calmer, more self-confident parents and enjoys the special attention he receives as the baby. He also has the advantage of learning from and modeling his adored older sibling who can do a handstand and even read him a story. However, he often feels terribly inadequate because he cannot do as much as she can. Unfortunately, he lacks the understanding that the problem has to do with their age difference, not with a basic flaw in him. A secondborn child often feels jealous because his older sibling is always accomplishing new firsts. He feels dominated by his older sister, who tries to maintain her number one position by always criticizing him and telling him what to do. He often feels rejected by her and left out because with her superior verbal abilities and her ongoing new ventures, she monopolizes their parents' attention. He, too, feels angry but has trouble asserting himself with his stronger, more physically and verbally adept older sister.

The middle child gains from some of the positives of being both a younger and an older sibling. She has an older sibling to learn from, who can watch over her, and she has a younger sibling who looks up to her, whom she can nurture. But as a middle child she faces some of her own unique challenges. She feels upset about losing her role as the baby, and often feels left out and jealous because both her older and younger siblings command so much attention. She is extremely competitive with her siblings, too. She is constantly chasing after the older one to try and catch up with him, while rushing to stay ahead of the younger one who is closing in on her from behind. The middle child has another tough dilemma. She is not the oldest and not the youngest, so she must struggle to established her own identity.

Though these reactions seem natural and common enough, on a daily basis they can cause children to feel bad about themselves, angry with their parents and siblings, and even unloved.

Parents often miss what is going on. Sometimes this happens because they are too busy, or so unfamiliar with birth order issues that they cannot decipher what they see. Children often have such a hard time comprehending what they are feeling and putting their emotions into words that they cannot tell their parents what is bothering them, either. Sometimes, they are afraid to tell because they fear that their emotions are bad (how can they feel jealous of a brother?), especially if the adults have not been very accepting of these emotions. So they hold them in, instead. But holding in emotions can cause children to feel much internal pain and even depression.

Often when children are distraught, however, they will act out their emotions, as Sam did when he ripped Elizabeth's pictures off the wall. This negative behavior can then start up an unfortunate chain of events. The parents might react impulsively, yell at or punish the child, and never get to the bottom of the issue, leaving him feeling unsupported, misunderstood, and even angrier. He may even act up worse, bringing on yet another round of unhappy interactions with his parents. In the end, the child feels alone and miserable and the parents feel distant from their child and incompetent. And so family life carries on with all these unresolved feelings smoldering under the surface until the next incident occurs and these undying embers fuel the blaze.

When you become aware of each of your children's birth order issues, identify them when they arise, and learn how to intervene, you can really make a difference in your children's lives. You must also learn which of your own behaviors contribute to your children's problems, and how to avoid them. Once you understand the issues and become actively involved by using a positive phrase or action, you can help your children to overcome their problems. This book will show you how.

I first describe daily life through the eyes of a firstborn, secondborn, middleborn, only child, and a twin. You will see why each child feels a certain way, how his emotions affect his behavior, and how you can be of help. Please note that the relationships that I have discussed between the firstborn and the secondborn child can occur between any older and younger child in the family. I have discussed the twin experience because twins relate to each other in much the same way as any two siblings do, and even when they are born only moments apart, they establish their own special birth order. I have also included a chapter on only children because they, too, occupy a unique spot in a family. They are firstborn children without siblings.

In each chapter, a particular child (or two children in the case of twins) will represent a certain birth order position. Each child, whether a girl or a boy, is a composite of all the other children in that particular position that I have ever spoken with or heard about. Like characters in a play, they will bring to life the full flavor of their unique experience.

In fact, in the first three chapters, a real-life drama unfolds. We watch the natural development of a family as it grows from one to two to three children, and we see the effect these changes have upon each child.

Some of the children's emotions appear to overlap, such as experiencing rejection or feeling left out. Though these feelings seem to be only a hair's breadth away from each other, each actually casts a somewhat different hue in the spectrum of emotions, so it is treated separately.

As you read, you may find that some of the feelings and behaviors described in a chapter may apply to your child, while others may not. You will see that some of the feelings, such as jealousy, will show up in most chapters. This is because all children feel jealousy in their sibling relationships. However, in the middle child chapter, for instance, jealousy will be discussed in terms of what causes a middle child to feel that way. But you can certainly use some of the same strategies to help all of your children deal with the same emotion.

Following a description of each emotion, there is a section entitled "The Effect on the Child's Development." Here, I describe some ways in which the particular emotional experience might affect the child later on in life if the child's parents do not intervene.

I must strongly emphasize that these hypothetical outcomes are being presented not to forecast any definitive character traits, but only to alert you to the urgency of intervening when your child is young, so that you can help prevent these kinds of problems from developing. These possible results are also being presented to show you how your child's early emotional experiences can be played out in other areas of life, for example, at school or with friends, so that they can be easily identified and worked with, if and when they do occur.

Each chapter also has a "What Parents Can Do" section. Here, I offer specific suggestions on how to work with your child on a particular issue. You will find helpful phrases that you can use to provide your children with the crucial support and reassurance that they need. I believe this is one of the best ways to help a child. I also suggest different strategies for various situations and give some specific skills that you can teach your child to use that will improve her relationship with her siblings and help her to cope on her own. Keep in mind that it will take time for your family to integrate these approaches and see the results.

Later chapters describe some specific factors such as the size of the family, sibling age, and gender differences, and show how they can affect the child's birth order experience. We see what life is like for the oldest child when she has to share her parents with two, three, or even six younger siblings instead of just one; whether a secondborn child only two years younger than his older sibling will feel more competitive with her than if they were spaced six years apart; and if a middle child who is the only one of his gender feels less needy for attention. We also take a look at ways in which boys and girls are treated differently in their families.

I give some recommendations about how to minimize the difficulties that these factors can create and, in particular, specific steps to take to ensure that your sons and daughters feel equally loved and valued.

Special attention is paid to how the parents' birth order experience affects their relationship with their child. That's because it has such a strong impact upon the parent-child relationship, upon how parents feel about themselves, and how they get along in life. If you are a firstborn child, for instance, you will find out under what circumstances you are most likely to identify with your firstborn child and be more sympathetic toward him and on the other hand, when this identification might cause you to react negatively. You will also become aware of the possibility that you might treat a child from another birth order position exactly the way you treated your sibling in that position, and the kinds of difficulties a couple faces when each spouse comes from the same or a different birth order. This chapter is designed to give you a deeper understanding of your own emotions and behaviors and assist you in managing your relationships and your life more successfully.

There certainly are other factors that can affect the child's birth order experience, including the quality of the parent-child relationship (is a parent angry or loving?), the child's temperament (is he generally easygoing or more intense?), the family's socioeconomic status, and family issues such as coexisting with stepsiblings or half siblings (which can upset the birth order and even cause a firstborn child to become the youngest). However, there are far too many variables to cover in depth in this book and what is presented here are some of the most basic factors affecting the birth order experience.

By understanding how all these factors affect a child's daily experience, and by following the suggestions in the book, you can help your child to have a happier life.

The Firstborn Child

Barely visible, seven-year-old Rachel and four-year-old Michael sit immersed in a bathtub full of bubbles. They are busily giving each other soap hairdos. When some soap gets in Michael's eye and he begins to cry, Rachel carefully wipes it for him with a washcloth.

As Michael has grown, he has become a very enjoyable companion for Rachel. She has fun playing hide-and-seek with him and giving him horsey rides throughout the house. She never needs to feel lonely. Michael is always there, willing and eager to play. She has fun making up games for them, and Michael will usually follow her lead. He will be her pupil when they play school, the game show host when she is the contestant, and at times her little baby.

Not only is he an amenable playmate but he is an adoring one. Early on Michael showed great affection for Rachel. When he was only a tiny baby, he would light up each time she walked in the room. In fact, she was the one he smiled most for; she was dubbed "the smile expert." Now when she arrives home from school, he races to her and hugs her before she has a chance to put down her book bag. Michael's affection makes Rachel feel very special.

Rachel loves her brother Michael. She used to pat and kiss

Mommy's tummy when he was still inside. She could not wait until he was born. "When is he going to come out?" she would ask impatiently. And then, there he was. So tiny, so fragile. He smelled so good. She decided it was her job to protect him and take care of him (after all, she was bigger).

When he was crying, she would run to get him his favorite musical clown to cheer him up. At times, she seemed to understand him better than the adults. Once when he was screeching and Grandma and Grandpa did not know what to do, she pulled off his socks and tickled his feet, and she got him to start laughing. One night when their parents went out and Michael was sad, Rachel held him on her lap for the entire evening. Whenever someone starts fighting with Michael in the playground, she runs in between them and pushes the other child away.

At night, Rachel likes to read her brother stories and teach him how to recognize letters. She shows him how to keep his ankles straight when they are ice-skating and how to turn the cassette over in the tape recorder. When he gets it right, she feels proud.

As the firstborn child, Rachel has benefited tremendously from being the sole focus of her parents' love and attention for three years. She feels a strong identification with them, and they have taught her a great deal. Now, it is through her relationship with Michael that Rachel is learning how to be a caretaker, to share, to be empathic, to take charge, and to be responsible. This experience will help her build her self-confidence and become a reliable friend, spouse, mentor, leader, and parent. Her relationship with Michael can be a close and rewarding one for her, for the rest of her life.

But as much as she adores Michael, she has ambivalent feelings about being an older sibling. As we shall see, she harbors some angry feelings about Michael's birth, and at times she feels jealous, pressured by her parents, intruded upon, resentful, and angry.

"Am I Good Enough?"

🐝 *"Rachel, you only got a ninety-seven on your spelling test. What happened to the other three points?"*

As first-time parents, Rachel's parents were very excited, yet very intense about their new role. They made sure that they had researched and purchased the most high-tech car seat, crib, and high chair for their baby. Rachel's room (the former office) was repapered with a tiny duck and bunny print, and a developmentally correct black and white mobile was hung over the crib. Her parents read all the most up-to-date books and articles on pregnancy and attended the most widely acclaimed childbirth classes. The push was on for them to be the best parents possible, if not to do the job perfectly.

Once Rachel was born, every cry, smile, and bowel movement received great attention. As she grew, her progress became extremely important to her parents. Did her height and weight fall into the right percentile? Was she crawling or sitting on schedule like their friends' children? In fact, as first-time parents, they had the time and a strong desire to stimulate Rachel's growth and took great pleasure when she seemed advanced. That's why firstborns tend to walk and talk earlier than later borns.

New parents cherish their baby and, above all, want her to be happy. They often have a secret, or not so secret, wish for her to do well in every sphere of her life, academically, socially, and emotionally. She should feel good about herself, have tons of friends, and, of course, go to Harvard. She should be independent, honest, brave, and polite.

Inexperienced and insecure about how to help their child to achieve these goals, they may push her to read by the age of three, overbook her in after-school programs, and endlessly drill her in math once she starts grade school. Unfamiliar with how children naturally behave, they may establish overly demanding, inappropriate rules for her behavior, such as "You can only ask for one treat a day" (so she will not be spoiled), "You must do your home-work without any help" (so she will be independent), and "You can't cry when you strike out" (so she will be strong). Unfortunately, she may be criticized or punished frequently for failing to comply with these difficult standards.

After a younger sibling is born, parents often pressure their older child harder to behave well because they need her cooperation and so that she will "set a good example" for the younger one. Most parents forget just how little the older one is and often expect her to act more maturely than her age. Parents will openly admit, "From the minute we came home with our infant, we no longer saw our two-year-old as a baby."

Parental pressure can stem from other sources, as well. Especially with the firstborn, it is common for parents to view the child as a narcissistic extension or a reflection of themselves. If Rachel walks or talks early, she is good, so her parents are good. Later on in life, if Rachel wins the spelling bee or achieves a high score on her SATs, her parents feel successful—so they prod her along.

As they raise their children, parents are also unconsciously (or consciously) trying to fulfill their own unresolved need to feel valuable in life. If one (or both) of Rachel's parents felt unloved or inadequate in any way as a child, or still does, he or she may hope to achieve worthiness through Rachel's achievements.

For example, if Rachel's father was labeled a poor student or not good at sports, he may try to fix this view of himself by insisting that Rachel achieve only hundreds on her tests or hit only home runs at Little League. He may even overreact to normal developmental issues such as Rachel's resistance to writing sentences with her spelling words or her difficulty in connecting with the ball, and jump to the conclusion that she, too, will fail. As a result, he may get angry at Rachel for being like him, angry at himself for not preventing this from happening, and he may pressure Rachel even harder. The likelihood of such a pattern developing is even greater if the parent demands much of himself.

If a parent was dubbed a child prodigy in music but never became a musician as she planned, or felt that excelling in English was crucial to her sense of identity, she may try to coerce her child to take up where she left off.

Effect on the Child's Development

If Rachel is highly pressured as she grows, there may be some unfortunate repercussions. Though she will get the positive message that it is good to succeed, she may also believe that her value in life is tied to her performance. Only if she gets an "A" on her book report will she be loved. (Heaven forbid she gets an A-!) As a result, like many older siblings, she will, in fact, become a high achiever, but at a price. She may become a workaholic, have an overwhelming need to stay at the top, and feel very stressed much of the time, all to please her parents.

Internalizing her parents' voices and demands as all children do, Rachel may go through life as her own worst critic. When she makes a mistake or fails to achieve a goal, she may become furious with herself, and even suffer from low self-esteem. Rachel may extend this harsh approach toward others, including her spouse, her employees, and her children.

Some firstborn children go through life feeling that they cannot measure up to the high standards their parents expected; they may get very depressed. Lacking in confidence, they might drop out and refuse to compete altogether because they fear failure or because they feel very enraged by all the pressure that has been placed upon them. (That will show their parents!) The individual may decide the price for love is too high. If the parents have made all the decisions for the child ("You will be a doctor"), the child may grow up not knowing who she is and what she really would like to do. Adults with these issues often become perpetual students, drift from career to career, and never really settle down.

If the parent-child relationship is filled with constant criticism, battles, and nonacceptance, it will be a very unhappy one. The child will end up feeling insecure in the relationship and full of rage about the constant rejections. If the parents are less judgmental and demanding of a younger sibling, the firstborn will feel very resentful toward her sibling and even angrier at her parents.

What Parents Can Do

Give your child unconditional love. The firstborn child needs to feel that she is loved unconditionally. She will be happier and more successful in life if she feels loved and good about herself. You can help to ensure that this will happen in many ways.

Avoid criticizing your child. You should be careful not to improve upon everything your firstborn says and does ("Your bed is not neat enough!" or "Stand up tall!"). You should avoid comparing him to others ("Why can't you get good grades like your cousin?" or "Even your brother can catch a ball"). You must be patient and praise him often (positive reinforcement is the best form of encouragement). For example, when he is spelling a word, give him time to figure it out, rather than getting annoyed with him or jumping in with the answer. When he succeeds, tell him, "Good job" or "I like the way you sounded that word out," instead of saying, "Good boy." In this way, you will emphasize the distinction between his performance and his value as a person.

Convey a positive message about learning. If your child gets a low test score, rather than berate her, you might ask, "Do you understand the material?" or "Can we help you in any way?" The most important values that a parent should advance about school and other endeavors such as sports and the arts are these: it is pleasurable to learn, it makes a person feel good, one does not have to perform perfectly, and it is really the child's domain. These messages will help children to become self-motivated and less focused on pleasing others.

Break down difficult tasks. If he is having trouble learning a new skill, such as juggling, break the activity down into simpler parts for him. For example, "Let's just practice throwing one ball in the air." If he makes a mistake and becomes anxious, support him by saying, "Don't worry! You'll get it. Juggling is hard." You should openly admit when a task is hard for you or when you make a mistake. In this way you communicate that no one is perfect. This will promote a more relaxed attitude on the child's part.

Avoid negative phrases. When she leaves her pajamas on the floor for the umpteenth time, choose your words carefully. Avoid using phrases such as "What's the matter with you?" or "How many times have I told you not to," or negative adjectives such as dumb, stupid, lazy, and clumsy. These words pack a mighty wallop to the child's self-esteem and communicate that if the child makes a mistake, the parent will withdraw his or her love. You should relate to the child's behavior and restate the rules instead: "Pajamas need to go in the hamper." When you phrase it in this way, you are communicating that she is good, but her behavior must change. Over time, after much repetition, the child will internalize the rules on her own.

Be in tune with your child's interests. If either parent had unfulfilled aspirations of becoming a dancer or a scientist, and the child shows no desire to be involved in these areas at all, he should not be coerced. He might take up these interests on his own at a later point, or decide that swimming is the love of his life. You must always be in tune with your child and help him to cultivate his own interests while exposing him to new activities and ideas from time to time.

Explain why you pressure her. You might clarify for your first-born child why you pressure her more than her brother. Explain to her that parents often push their older child more because it is their first experience at being a parent. You are trying very hard to do a good job so that she will have a good life. However, you realize that you can give her a difficult time. When she feels that you are pushing her too hard, she should tell you.

Raise your awareness of your own personal issues involved. It is crucial that each parent try to identify when his or her own personal emotional issues are affecting the relationship with the child. For example, if you find yourself screaming hysterically at your child about cleaning up his room, examine your motivation. Were you labeled "the slob" in your family because you kept a messy room? Are you trying to protect your child from the same fate? Are you trying to repair your own image by keeping your home organized? If so, you must step back emotionally from your child and take a more objective approach. You cannot expect that a young child's room will always be neat. Rather than yelling, help your son organize his room so that it will be easier to maintain (each toy should have its place).

All parents should try to read and attend workshops to learn as much as they can about children's natural development. The more they comprehend about what is appropriate to expect from their child at a given age, the less they will pressure her.

"When Are You Going to Send That New Baby Back?"

🌿 *Mommy is reading Michael his bedtime story. Rachel plops down on the bed next to them and wants to join in. Within moments, Rachel has chosen the book that they will read and is fighting Michael for Mommy's lap. "Stop!" says Mommy. "I have two legs and enough room for both of you."*

Before Michael was born, Rachel had Mommy and Daddy's undivided attention. But as soon as her parents brought Michael home there were big changes. Rachel suddenly had to wait for every-thing. "Just one minute," Daddy would say when he was busy with Michael's bath and Rachel wanted him to put on a video for her. "You have to wait," Mommy would tell her when she was hungry and wanted a snack. Saddest of all were the evenings when one of her parents would announce, "I can't read to you tonight. Michael is very cranky and I have to calm him down."

Suddenly most of her parents' attention was focused on the baby. Mommy seemed to be feeding him all the time. When she did, Michael was so close to Mommy as he lay there sucking at her breast. Rachel felt left out.

Rachel began to worry that because her parents spent so much time with Michael they must love him more. Not only were Mommy and Daddy less available, but they were often angry with her, too. When she squeezed the baby too hard or tried to pick him up on her own, they scolded her. Instead of calmly reminding her to put her socks in the hamper, her overtired, overwrought parents snapped at her. There seemed to be fewer smiles and praises and more disapproval in their faces.

Like other children, Rachel often feared that Mommy and Daddy had had the baby to replace her and wondered why she was not good enough. One day she threw her teddy bear into Daddy's gym bag and headed for the door. When asked where she was going, she retorted, "To find a new family to love me."

She often got angry at her parents for bringing Michael into the family. Sometimes Rachel would pinch Michael when no one was looking, take away his pacifier to make him cry, or throw her doll at Daddy while he was dressing Michael. Rachel yearned to have her parents to herself again. She didn't want to share them anymore. Her main mission in life became to regain her parents' attention. When Mommy was breast-feeding, Rachel would jump on the sofa or climb up on the counter to try to make her mad and get her to stop taking care of Michael. Sometimes she fought her parents in more subtle, seemingly unrelated ways such as saying "butt-head" because her parents considered it to be rude, or refusing to zip up her jacket. (Even negative attention seemed better than none.) However, the more angry her parents became with her, the more abandoned and alone she felt.

Now, even though Rachel and Michael are older, Rachel still struggles to be the center of attention. Sometimes she will start an argument with her parents by refusing to clean her room or to get dressed by herself, because it keeps them focused on her. When Daddy arrives home from work, Rachel outruns Michael screaming, "I'm first," and gets in the first hug, leaving poor Michael dissolved in tears. At dinner she talks nonstop, preventing Michael from getting a word in edgewise.

Ironically, many parents feel that they spend lots more time with their older child than their younger one, especially at the beginning when they are helping her with her adjustment. But to Rachel, any time spent with Michael can be experienced as time (or love) taken away from her, and it feels like too much. And so she has creatively invented at least 101 insidious ways to take the attention away from Michael.

Effect on the Child's Development

The loss of being the center of attention after the birth of a sibling is often called displacement or dethronement by theorists (because the child has lost his "throne"). Like any loss, this causes children to feel sad and angry, and in this case, jealous, too. It is such a powerful experience for children that many adults have repressed their feelings about the event entirely. Other adults will acknowledge that they still feel angry at their parents for having had another child. Apparently, the painful feelings about the sibling's birth often resonate throughout the individual's life.

As Rachel grows, she might try to be the center of attention wherever she goes and find it intolerable when she is not. At school, she may constantly raise her hand to answer all of the questions so that the teacher will focus only on her, have a hard time sharing her best friend, or act very bossy with her playmates. As an adult, she may feel an overwhelming need to be the one in charge (the director or owner of a business) to ensure that her position and importance is secure. She may also try to dominate family life by controlling discussions, creating crises, or attempting to make all the family decisions. This need to be the center of attention and to be in control often leaves no room for others and can push people away.

If, on the other hand, she believes that she has no chance in the world to retrieve the limelight, like many older siblings, she may instead draw inward and fade into the background.

What Parents Can Do

Be alert to your child's reaction. Parents love their firstborn child dearly. They want him to make an easy adjustment to his sibling and form a good relationship with her, especially if the parents were older siblings themselves or had difficult sibling relationships. These wishes can cause them to deny that he is really upset about the sibling's birth. Though there are definitely varying degrees of reactions to a new brother or sister, every child struggles with feelings of anger, sadness, and jealousy, and when unresolved, these emotions can linger throughout life. By addressing the feelings directly, you can alleviate a great deal of your child's distress.

Tell your child the family story. You can help your firstborn tremendously by telling her the "family story," in this way: "When you were very little, it was just you and Mommy and Daddy in the family and we had lots of time to spend together. Then there was a change in the family. Your brother was born and you had to share Mommy and Daddy's love and attention. We know that that was very hard for you, and that it still is, at times. It is difficult for any child to be the older child and share her parents' love. It is hard for younger children, too. Children often feel angry and sad about this. When you feel this way and you want more attention, you can come and tell us. You can say, 'I feel angry' or 'I want attention,' and we will try to help you. But remember always that we have enough love for both of our children and no one could ever take your place in our hearts." This approach helps the child gain insight into what she is feeling and reassures her that you truly love and understand her. She will need to protest less through negative behaviors because she can express herself openly.

Explain that babies need extra care. You should also explain to him that since his sister was born, you have had to spend a great deal of time taking care of her to keep her safe and healthy, and that this is because she is too little to do very much for herself, not because you love her more. When he was younger, you took care of him in the same way. To reassure him, you can show him baby pictures of him being fed in his high chair or pushed in his stroller.

Acknowledge her feelings. When you are busy with the younger child's bedtime routine and the older one is having a hard time waiting for you to help her with her homework or read her a story, you should acknowledge her feelings. You might say, "We know that it's hard to wait, but we will be right with you." You might also try to include her in his care in some way (if she is willing).

Involve your child in problem solving. It can also relieve both parent and child if the parent talks about the dilemma of parenting two children and engages the child in joint problem solving. For example, "This is hard for me. I really want to help you, but your sister needs me, too. What shall we do?" Often the child will save the day by suggesting something that the parent has already taught him, such as "I'll finish my spelling homework, then when you're done reading her a story, you can help me with my math" or "Just come and give me a quick hug." Some parents find that setting a timer for ten minutes can help quell the anxiety of a waiting child.

The length of the wait is finite! As hard as it is, you must also try to divide your time and attention between your children as evenly as possible.

Help her understand her negative attention-seeking behaviors. The older child needs help in understanding that at times she uses negative attention-seeking behavior to focus the attention upon herself (e.g., when she disrupts her brother's storytelling at the dinner table). When this occurs, you should describe what has happened ("Joey was telling us a story about his trip to the firehouse and you started to kick him"), help her see the connection between her feelings and her behavior ("You were feeling angry, so you kicked Joey"), and address the underlying issue ("It seems that it is hard for you to share Mommy and Daddy's attention with Joey"). Then, you must set a limit on her negative behavior and encourage her to verbalize her feelings. "It is okay to be angry, but you cannot hurt Joey. Next time, you must use your words instead and let us know how you feel."

Create opportunities for positive interactions. If your child frequently resorts to negative behaviors to gain attention and your relationship is chock-full of stressful interactions, you can slowly turn things around over time by talking with him about his feelings and making sure to find moments to smile at him, hug him, and praise him. Spending time alone with the child is the most important way to reassure him that he is loved. Words alone are simply not enough. When the parent takes the time to sit down and ask about his day, or takes a walk with him, this communicates to the child, "I want to be with you, you are valuable to me, and I really care about you." The child ends up feeling more secure in the relationship and no longer needs to test the parent to see if he is loved.

Parents are often surprised, however, when even after a day of intensive quality time alone with their older child, he will complain when they return home and the parent embraces the younger child at the door. The older one is having a hard time relinquishing that special feeling of having the parent all to himself.

"Who Do You Love More?"

Grandma and Grandpa are videotaping Michael doing his latest moves from karate class. Rachel suddenly jumps up from the couch and launches into wild pirouettes, blocking Michael from the camera.

Rachel gets very jealous of Michael. Everyone always smiles at him and says, "He's so cute!" When they walk down the street, the neighbors, the storekeepers, and even Rachel's friends will chat with Michael or give him a special treat. Ever since he was little, he was always doing something new: rolling over, crawling across the room, saying his first word, and walking—to a family chorus of "oohs" and "ahs." Now he can tell funny knock-knock jokes, he can hang upside down on the monkey bars, and he can even sign his name on a birthday card, much to everyone's amazement. Rachel does not realize that she had her own "firsts" too and that she also got plenty of attention. She somehow does not equate the praise she receives for her current accomplishments with the praise that Michael gets.

As Michael grows, if he is particularly skilled in gymnastics, has more friends than Rachel, or seems to get along better with Mom and Dad, this will intensify her jealousy. Often parents will say that their secondborn is easier, and that they feel more relaxed the second time around. They may be unaware that they smile more at the younger one than at their more demanding, often more difficult older child. But Rachel notices!

Not only is Rachel envious of all the constant admiration that Michael receives, but she is envious that Michael continues to get more attention than she does with his daily care. Michael is often referred to as "the baby" of the family and the parents tend to "baby" him. They side with him more, ask less of him, and allow him to engage in behavior that for Rachel would be impermissible. At moments when everyone is focusing on Michael and treating him in special ways, Rachel often feels less important and even unloved.

As we saw in the preceding section on displacement, because she feels so painfully rejected, Rachel is intent on retrieving her number one position in the family. In an attempt to be loved the most, she uses her more mature intellectual and physical abilities to compete with him. In an effort to one-up Michael, Rachel constantly rolls her eyes at him and criticizes his ideas ("You're wrong. The dog we saw did not have spots on his ears"), diminishes his accomplishments ("That's not the way to draw a person"), or knocks his possessions ("What's so special about your new bicycle? Mine goes faster"). If Michael is being reprimanded for not picking up his toys, Rachel will try to show that her behavior is superior ("See Mommy! I cleaned up my whole room"). Rachel regularly taunts Michael by announcing, "Daddy and Mommy love me more than you"—anything to keep Michael number two.

Rachel also tries to control Michael. She must be the one to choose the games they will play, the television show they will watch, and even the snack that they will eat. If he will not cooperate, she will use her sophisticated language skills to manipulate him ("If you won't be my baby in the story, I won't let you join the circus with me when we grow up") or brute force (she sits on him until he agrees).

Rachel's maneuvers can become even more extreme if she feels threatened because her younger brother seems to be catching up to her in some way or if he can do something that she cannot and she worries he will surpass her. For example, if he is starting to overtake her in a race, she will trip him, or if he dares to recognize a word in her reader, and reading has been one of Rachel's claims to fame, she might yell at him, "You're stupid! You'll never learn to read."

Effect on the Child's Development

As she grows, Rachel's need to be number one can become a major driving force for her. She may be highly competitive at school and have a hard time tolerating it when someone else receives higher grades, or become a workaholic on her job and feel demolished if someone receives the promotion she wanted.

Rachel may continue to compete with Michael for her parents' love for the rest of her life. She will keep accounts of how many times her parents visit her brother's home and compare her parents' praises for each set of grandchildren. She may try to outdo her brother by buying a bigger house or throwing a huge surprise party for her parents' anniversary.

Rachel may treat others as competitors, too. When she feels jealous, she may criticize her friend's new house ("Too bad it is so far from the train") or put her husband down ("That's not the way to wash Jimmy's hair"). These behaviors will injure her relationships.

Some firstborns run from competition instead, because they feel hopeless or because it seems too aggressive. It probably feels as if a childhood fantasy of harming their younger sibling is coming true. In such a case, the adult may feel inadequate, angry with herself for not trying, and unfulfilled in life.

What Parents Can Do

Explain why small children get attention. Your firstborn child needs your assistance in understanding that small children are very endearing to grown-ups. Everyone is watching them as they develop into "real" people and gets excited about the child's new abilities. When she was small, the whole family got excited about her new skills, too. In fact, they still do! Does she remember how thrilled Grandma and Grandpa were to hear her read from a book for the first time? Praise her for her more mature abilities, such as making her bed, or writing an interesting sentence with her spelling words, so that she will see that grown-up children are valued in the family as much as babies.

Convey acceptance for his jealousy. Reinforce the idea that it is normal to feel jealous. All children do. Emphasize that it is important that he tell you when he feels unhappy. He can say, "I'm jealous," or "I need attention, too," and you will help him. If you do not convey such acceptance, he will grow up feeling guilty about his jealous feelings, try hard to hide them, and feel bad about himself or act out in negative ways. Talking with children openly about their jealousy and providing them with reassurance ("You are both lovable and special") diminishes the pain that this emotion can cause.

Set limits if she dominates the younger one. Help your oldest child see that her domineering, critical behavior is caused by her jealous feelings and set limits with her. For example, if she is always telling her brother what to do, you might say, "You must take turns at choosing which game you will play," or "He doesn't have to be the baby if he doesn't want to." If she tells him, "You draw scribble-scrabble," you must tell her that she cannot say things that will hurt her brother's feelings and make him feel bad about himself.

Reassure him. When your firstborn seems threatened because his younger sister has started to ski on slopes of the same difficulty as him, and he is worried that she will surpass him, you can explain to him that his sister wants very much to be like him. Therefore, she tries hard to copy what he does. As a result, like other younger siblings, she will start doing things at a younger age than he did. He does not need to worry or try to hold her back—she can never take away his accomplishments or the love that you feel for him. There is room for two successful children in the family.

Avoid labeling or comparing your children. It is important to avoid inadvertently setting up a competition between the two children by using labels ("Oh! Your brother is the great sportsman of the family"), comparing the children ("Your sister isn't afraid to walk over and make friends. Why are you?"), or playing favorites with one child (by giving that one much more time and attention).

If you praise your older child for her talents and abilities, show her affection, and spend time alone with her, she will feel loved for who she is and will have less need to compete with her brother.

"Get Him Out of Here!"

🐝 *Rachel has her Barbie dolls spread out across her bedroom rug. She has spent an hour carefully dressing them, choosing their accessories, and positioning them at her pretend picnic. Suddenly, Michael walks in, starts moving everything around, and runs off with Ken. Rachel dissolves in tears.*

Though Michael has certainly enriched Rachel's life since his birth, in many respects he has been an intrusion. Rachel used to be alone with Mommy and Daddy and then Michael suddenly appeared and moved into her space. He has constantly interfered with her desires and taken time and attention away from her.

Initially, when he was a tiny infant, her parents were constantly busy with him and were frequently not able to come when she called. As soon as he started rolling across the living room floor and picking up toys, Rachel got wind of the idea that now he would start to get in her way physically, as well.

As he grew and began crawling, he shadowed her every move. He followed her into the kitchen, and out on the back porch, or insisted upon sitting next to her on the couch. She could hardly be alone. Though sometimes she felt flattered or treated this as a game, at other times it felt like a terrible nuisance and made her run the other way.

Michael began to get into her things, too. When she was playing with her tea set, Michael would crawl over and knock down any cups and saucers that were in his way. She tried to use her words as she had been instructed, and say, "No! Michael," but, like a Duracell baby, he kept on coming. Michael seemed to want anything that Rachel was playing with.

At the age of four, Michael still intrudes upon Rachel's life. When Rachel and a friend are having a game of checkers and Michael cannot join in, he may topple the board. And when the two girls want to play Cinderella alone, Michael will refuse to leave the room. If Rachel's friend finds Michael adorable and wants to play with him, Rachel will feel as if Michael is interfering in her relationship.

Michael often surreptitiously removes things from Rachel's drawers or shelves. One day Michael even found Rachel's diary and scribbled all over it. Because of his interference, Rachel often has to do her art projects sitting with her back to the door, forcing it shut. Her shrill cries, "Get him out of here. He's bothering me," are heard throughout the day.

Effect on the Child's Development

As she grows, Rachel may continue to find Michael's intrusion intolerable, especially during the teen years when she is super-focused on establishing her independence. Most of the time she will control her rage and simply abandon her activity, but sometimes Rachel may even punch or kick her brother when he interferes with a playdate, takes something from her room, or just gets in her way. Because she feels so protective of her space and possessions, she may react aggressively with her peers, too. In the playground, when another child takes her jump rope without asking, or grabs the swing that she is running for, she might push the culprit to the ground.

Later in life, though she no longer will react physically with others, she may become extremely argumentative when her classmate borrows her book without asking, or when her employer assigns another professional to work with her on a project that she has been happily conducting on her own.

Sometimes, the child's fear of her own aggression, her feeling of powerlessness to stop her younger sibling, or her anxiety about arousing disapproval from the adults can cause her to stand by passively in the face of an intrusive sibling and allow herself to be pushed around. When Michael wrecks her puzzle, she may pack it up rather than fight. This passive behavior may show up when she is a grown-up, too. Even though she does not want to, she may allow her spouse or her children to take over her computer when she is right in the middle of a project, leaving her feeling very vulnerable and unhappy.

If Rachel has been told that she must always share her things with Michael, either because the parents want their children to learn to share or to prevent Michael from having terrible tantrums, she may grow up feeling that she is not entitled to her own possessions. In fact, she might even feel selfish when she wants to buy herself something and frequently return home from a shopping trip empty-handed. Feeling that she is not allowed to have more than her sibling (or others), she may even give away her possessions (offer her bag of potato chips to her friends at lunch) to avoid feeling guilty. On the other hand, she may become extremely possessive instead and refuse to share at all.

Some older siblings grow up craving privacy. They will often say, "My life is an open door." Older siblings can feel that they simply do not have any time or space to be alone and suffer miserably, especially if they have been forced to watch a younger sibling all the time, belong to a large family, or share a room with a sibling.

Longing for solitude, an older sibling may lock her door, become a loner, or become superindependent to create space for herself. An adult older sibling may become very upset by having to share a dorm room at college, or by having her children underfoot all the time. She may not even know how to assert her need for privacy.

What Parents Can Do

Explain why the younger one follows him. You can help your firstborn child by explaining to him that his sister loves him and looks up to him. That's why she wants to be around him all the time and do what he is doing. But you must reassure him that you recognize his need for privacy.

Support her self-assertion. Encourage her to assert herself and teach her how. If she wants to be alone, she should tell her brother, "I need my privacy." If he will not listen, she can say, "It makes me angry when you don't respect my privacy," but she cannot hurt him. She must ask her parents or her caretaker for help, instead.

Encourage the younger one to give the older one privacy. You need to work with the younger child, too. Because she is younger, she probably does not understand her older brother's need. Explain to her that every person needs to be alone at times (even she likes to play alone in the bathtub with her sailboat). When her brother asks for privacy, she must respect him. It does not mean that he does not like her or that she did anything wrong.

Set up family rules. Establishing specific family rules or procedures about privacy, with the children's input, can help tremendously. If the children have their own rooms, each child must learn to knock before entering. You should model this behavior. If the two children share a room and one wants privacy, perhaps the other child can watch a video in the living room for a while. Or a quiet spot in the house such as the den or the parents' room can be used to provide a child with total privacy. Some parents set up a schedule whereby each child attends an after-school program or goes on a playdate once or twice a week on alternate days, leaving the room available to the other child.

Invite friends for your younger one. When the older child has a playdate, it would help if one of the other child's friends were to visit or you or the baby-sitter could plan a special activity with him to keep him occupied. The older child should be encouraged to include him sometimes, too, so he will not feel constantly rejected. Not only will this be beneficial for his self-esteem, but he will be more willing to grant his sister her privacy at other times. Some parents establish a rule whereby the older child can play for one hour alone with her guest and then the younger one must be included. To encourage the younger child's inclusion at times, you can initiate some group projects, such as making papier-mâché or providing the children with construction paper, glitter, sparkles, and glue for collages.

Do not coerce the older one to share his things. An older child should not be forced to let his younger sibling use his things. He has a right to have his own possessions and to make an independent choice about sharing. His sister must be instructed that she needs to ask her brother if she can use something of his and treat it carefully, if he agrees, and that he has a right to say no (and vice versa). When he is unwilling, he can tell her, "I don't feel like sharing right now." Though there is no question that he will often need some gentle coaxing to share at all, he should have opportunities to decline.

It is very positive to ask a child, "Would you like to share your pretzels with your sister?" rather than say, "Give her some pretzels right now!" If he refuses, just say, "Maybe next time," without instilling any guilt, or have the child put the snack away till later and explain to the other child, "Your sister does not feel like sharing right now." Having the choice will engender in him a willingness to share and make the experience more pleasurable.

Set up a separate space for each child. If siblings share a room, parents find it helpful to set up separate shelves or storage bins for each child's toys and books and an area for shared items. As the children grow, if they are interested, you might consider using a bookshelf or a screen to serve as a room divider, to help define each child's space.

Give them some communal property. To teach the children about sharing, you can give them some special communal property, such as a computer, and teach them how to take turns. Setting up a weekly calendar with times designated for each child's use each day and using a timer to monitor the length of time can be extremely helpful. The children will devise similar methods when they need to share in other situations, as well.

If you safeguard your older child's need for separateness and teach him how to negotiate his boundaries, he will feel less vulnerable and more comfortable in his relationships as he grows.

"It's Not Fair!"

🐝 *It's seven o'clock. The family has just finished dinner and Rachel is refusing to help Daddy clean off the table. "It's not fair!" she screams. Daddy is furious with Rachel, and is intent upon getting her to comply. Rachel is very resentful because she keeps catching glimpses of Michael, lounging around the living room watching a video.*

Because Michael is tinier and less developed, Rachel and Michael's parents are often very protective of him and more demanding of Rachel. As harried parents, they frequently give many responsibilities to Rachel, such as throwing out the garbage or stacking the dishwasher, while Michael is not required to do very much at all. While it is natural for Rachel to assume some family responsibilities as she gets older and it is, in fact, good for her growth, her parents need to deal with this issue very carefully. Otherwise, without their realizing it, in the course of daily life, Rachel may become very resentful.

At her age, Rachel must do certain chores to earn an allowance, but Michael seems to get everything he wants just by asking. Rachel is often asked to do Michael's chores, such as cleaning up his toys, when he refuses. This frequently occurs when two siblings share a room. Even when Michael does pitch in, Rachel commonly ends up doing the lion's share of the work. Totally unaware, the parents have established a different set of rules for each child, which feels terribly unfair to Rachel.

To make matters worse, Rachel is often asked to be responsible for Michael. Constant requests such as, "Watch him for a minute," "Keep an eye on your brother while I take a shower," or "Do me a favor, put the tape on for Michael," can raise resentment. Sometimes Rachel will retort angrily, "Why should I?" or "You had him, why do I have to take care of him!"

Rachel and Michael's parents tend to side with Michael whenever the two children are quarreling. This is probably because since Michael was born, they have had to protect him whenever Rachel was around. Rachel would try to put Michael's pacifier into his mouth when he didn't want it; climb into his cradle; or, at times, purposely try to harm him. Now when the two children are fighting in the next room, the parents will automatically yell, "Rachel, stop fighting with your brother." If Michael has instigated the quarrel by taking away Rachel's marker, Rachel will feel deeply wronged.

Rachel may also feel irate that Mom and Dad allow Michael to have Rollerblades at his age when they refused to let her do so until she was six even though she begged and pleaded, or that when both of the children are acting silly, their parents are harder on Rachel. "Your brother is younger. You should know better." Parents often reprimand the older one because they have high expectations for her, they need her to be good, and because they think that they can probably get her to change her behavior quicker than Michael. This happens so frequently that many older siblings will complain, "You hate me. You're always angry at me."

In general, Rachel and Michael's parents are stricter with Rachel than they are with Michael. That's because, as the firstborn child, Rachel has been involved in new areas that have raised questions and conflicts for her anxious, first-time parents, such as "Should she be allowed to go on a sleepover at her age?" Out of nervousness and insecurity, her parents have often responded by setting up rules that were too rigid, demanding, overprotective, inconsistent, and even arbitrary, for example, "You cannot go on a sleepover until you are ten."

More relaxed because they have already experienced these dilemmas and everyone survived and thrived, they may loosen up their rules and their attitude with Michael, and he may not be punished at all for the same misbehaviors. However, the strict rules and pressure continue for Rachel, who proceeds to make forays into new territories. As Rachel compares her treatment with Michael's, she is furious.

Effect on the Child's Development

If Rachel believes that she is always required to do more, is reprimanded more, and that Michael generally receives preferential treatment, she can grow up feeling extremely resentful and even unloved. In response, she might fight her parents constantly about everything they ask her to do, from putting her sneakers away to doing her homework, or take out her frustration on her siblings through physical aggression or emotional jabs, provocations, putdowns, and criticisms. "It's not fair," may become her battle cry.

If Rachel believes that her parents will respond angrily when she expresses her emotions, or senses that no one cares to listen to her at all, she may instead hold these painful feelings inside and become withdrawn, sullen, and even depressed. Feeling powerless to change the situation, she may become passive-aggressive and seek subtle ways to express her rage, such as "forgetting" to set the table or leaving her dirty socks on the bathroom floor.

Some firstborns resolve their situation by doing whatever they are told, repressing any resentment they may feel and becoming superdependable and cooperative, especially if they receive praise for their behavior or if the younger one presents big behavioral problems to the family. It is also common for children to shift dramatically from one of these modes of behavior to another, depending upon the moment.

As Rachel grows, her unresolved feelings of resentment from childhood may reemerge whenever she perceives she is being mistreated by others in a similar way. For example, when she finds herself doing most of the work on a group science project at school, or when her husband is not doing an equal share of the household chores, she may explode. Her anger may surface most directly when she is caring for her own children. If she always had to clean up after her younger sibling, she may become enraged when her own child refuses to pick up his toys, especially if her child is the same sex as her sibling. In her professional life, she may feel put upon when her boss asks her to stay beyond five o'clock, or to pick up an extra account that belonged to a coworker.

Rachel may also naturally assume most of the responsibility in situations because she is used to it, she is good at it, and she enjoys the acclaim she receives, even when she knows she is taking on too much (always volunteering to chair the committee). Her strong wish to be needed and loved may make it difficult for her to establish her boundaries by saying no, and she may walk through life frequently feeling overburdened, burned out, and resentful.

What Parents Can Do

Listen to her point of view. You can help your firstborn child most by listening to her and acknowledging her emotions. Make sure that you do not try to talk her out of her feelings because you feel guilty or angry. When she complains, try to step into her shoes and see how your actions may be affecting her. For example, if she

is upset because every morning you help her brother put his clothes on, but she must always dress herself, you might tell her, "I can see that my dressing your brother and not you seems unfair." This statement conveys an understanding while encouraging her to express herself openly. Giving her an explanation, such as "Small children have a hard time dressing themselves, so your brother needs my help," is crucial. While you obviously cannot change the objective reality, your support will make her feel better.

Treat your children equitably. Try to behave with your children in as equitable a fashion as possible. For example, it is important that both children are included in family tasks. As little as the youngest is, there might be something she can do. When she is really too little to do a task, you can explain to her brother that when he was little, he didn't fold the laundry or set the table either.

Explain why you need her help. You can further support her by explaining, "It is hard to be the older child in the family. You are stronger and understand what needs to be done, so we ask more of you. It is not because we love your brother more. When you were four, you also could not help out very much. As your brother grows up, he will do more."

Include all children in cleanup. If your firstborn becomes enraged because his younger sister picks up one toy during cleanup and then runs off, you must intervene. You might walk her back to the room and work with her to encourage her to participate ("Let's see how many blue blocks you can pick up," or "Let's do it together").

Always address your older child courteously. When her help is needed, you might say, "I'm very busy. Can you please help your brother with his shirt?" (it is not her obligation) or "I'm sorry that I have to interrupt your game." These statements convey respect for her independence and invite her cooperation. Praise her and show appreciation for her help. You might even plan to have a special dinner out with her or buy her something she has been longing for as a show of gratitude.

If she's already been asked for ten favors, you can say, "I'm sorry that I have to ask you for more help." It is important to compromise with her ("How about helping your brother brush his teeth during the commercial?"), offer her choices ("Before we leave, we need to clean off the table and pack the lunches. Which task would you like to do?"), and allow her to say no at times, so that she will learn how to assert her needs.

Monitor the way he participates in the family. If he starts to take over for his sister unnecessarily and is always doing too much, you should reassure him that he does not have to do it all to be loved. If, on the other hand, he refuses to cooperate when asked to help carry in the groceries, try to determine the reason. Maybe you've been asking too much of him lately or he is angry about something unrelated (he is jealous because his sister got a new bicycle).

Address all children in a quarrel. If the children are fighting in the next room, it is important to address both of them when asking them to stop, or to walk in and ascertain what has happened. Be open to hearing each child's viewpoint. When the children are making noise in the backseat of the car, never single out one child. Make a general statement instead, such as "You both need to sit quietly. Noise in a car is very dangerous for the driver." If the two children are out of control and need a time out, be sure to send each of them to a quiet spot.

Explain why the younger one gets privileges sooner. You should acknowledge how difficult it is for an older child to deal with a younger one's privileges. Explain to her that it is common for secondborn siblings to be allowed to ride a two-wheeler or go on a sleepover at an earlier age than firstborns because you've gone through the experience before and are more comfortable.

"I Can't Stand That Kid"

Rachel is frantically searching for her new necklace. She finds it lying on Michael's bed with the string broken and all the beads scattered. Enraged, she walks over to where Michael is playing on the floor and kicks over the block skyscraper that he is building.

As we have seen, at times Rachel is very angry about Michael's birth, the amount of attention he receives, his intrusion upon her life, parental pressure, and perceived inequities in her treatment. Early in her role as an older sibling, anger became a very difficult emotion for her.

As soon as her parents brought Michael home, they began warning Rachel not to hurt the baby. Whenever she tried to touch his soft hair or put a blanket on him, everyone hovered close by to make sure she would not harm him. When she felt jealous and poked him hard in the cheek, or sat on him while he was lying on the bed, she was screamed at. And what happened when Rachel (accidentally?) knocked Michael down when he was a toddler and he actually bled! She was probably met with tremendous outrage and rejection from her frightened parents and felt guilty and terrified by the destructive power of her rage.

Since the underlying cause of Rachel's aggression to begin with was the fear of losing her parents' love, their rejection left Rachel feeling more frightened, abandoned, and even angrier. If her rage was aimed directly at her parents instead (the true culprits for bringing Michael in), and she hit them or refused to listen, the outcome was probably the same. Feeling alone and upset, Rachel may have become even more confrontational in a desperate attempt to get some attention, withdrawn into herself, or tried to relinquish her aggression altogether.

It is not easy for a young child who lacks mature impulse control to contain her anger toward a younger sibling. Think about how much restraint it would take her, when she feels so mad, to glide her hand over the baby's arm to make nice, rather than hit him. At the same time that she is trying to restrict her behavior, she must endure her younger sibling's aggression, whether as an infant he is pulling her hair out of curiosity, as a toddler he is hitting or biting her because he has not yet learned to use words, or as a four-year-old he takes her new stickers to provoke her. Because she loves her parents so much, she is trying hard to incorporate their belief in nonaggression, an ideal that they tried to instill in her long before Michael arrived on the scene.

As a result, many firstborns learn to sit on their anger as they grow and even find it hard to assert themselves, and their wrath often gets expressed in more subtle ways. While some children will continue to knock their younger sibling down, especially when no one is looking (some children actually do remain openly aggressive), more often they may upset their sibling by withholding a toy, calling him a name, or refusing to let the younger one join in on a game.

In an attempt to cope with their anger, some children employ a psychological defense called "reaction formation" that transforms the anger into very strong caring, because it is more acceptable. Parents will comment, "Oh she just loves her brother to death," because she hugs him constantly, even if it is a little too hard, or "She is such a good sister. She cries bitterly when he falls down." While she may truly be concerned, she may also be worried that her angry thoughts caused his fall. Though there are genuine loving feelings in the relationship, the child may be overdoing it at times to hide her age. Although this defense mechanism can have some positive adaptive value for her, she also needs to deal with any angry feelings that she may be experiencing, rather than repress them.

Older children will often boss their younger sibling around, criticize him, and put him down when they are feeling rageful. This behavior will be enhanced if the parents relate to their children in this way. Some may try to get the younger one in trouble by encouraging him to say "stupid" to their parents, or to draw with Mommy's lipstick on the bathroom wall. If an older sibling has been successful at keeping the family focused on her by arguing when she is feeling angry, she may fight her parents tooth and nail over a small request such as hanging up her jacket.

Effect on the Child's Development
Deep inside, Rachel may carry much unresolved anger about Michael and being an older sibling. Whenever she feels jealous, intruded upon, pressured, or unfairly treated, these buried feelings may reemerge.

If she was a child who expressed her rage by bullying her younger sibling physically or emotionally, she may continue this tactic with him and others as she grows. She might continue to tickle her brother long after he tells her to stop, knock a younger child down in the park when he is in her way, or get into physical brawls when someone tags her out at Little League and she feels it is unfair. As an adult, she may become highly volatile if her spouse or her child will not do exactly what she wants, criticize a fellow employee with whom she is in competition, or explode when she feels mistreated by her boss or even by a waiter. If she has customarily started arguments to focus attention on herself, she may be the one who always starts fights at Thanksgiving dinner, or rants and raves at the annual company board meeting. This aggressive side of her personality can isolate her and seriously harm her personal and professional relationships.

If Rachel has instead learned to hold back her anger because she fears disapproval or the destructive power of her rage, she may refuse to fight back or feel unable to when she is being pushed around by others. She may even attempt to make her case, but back down immediately when challenged. If she does not express her emotions, she will end up feeling very vulnerable to others and constantly enraged.

But anger always needs a place to go. Rachel may turn the anger against herself where it feels safer (no one will get angry with her and it protects the person she is mad at). Unfortunately, she may suffer inside because she believes that she is very bad and unlovable because of her aggression. She may even grow up believing that her hostile thoughts or wishes can cause harm to someone, and if someone she is furious with actually does get hurt (e.g., a younger sibling breaks his leg), she will blame herself.

If, as a child, Rachel has expressed her anger in a passive-aggressive fashion, she may continue to do so throughout life. For example, she might call her brother a name and then scream for help when he retaliates, allow her grades to slip, or repeatedly come late to work. Though the goal of this behavior is to retaliate against the person who has wronged her, in reality these actions will injure Rachel most of all.

As we can see, the way in which Rachel copes with her anger will greatly affect her well-being in life. Rachel's parents must help her by teaching her how to deal with this emotion effectively early on.

What Parents Can Do

Talk openly about anger. It is crucial to create an environment in your home in which your firstborn child feels comfortable enough to talk openly about her angry feelings because she knows you will support her. You must also intervene if she is physically or emotionally bullying her brother. Acknowledge her feelings while setting a limit on her aggressive behavior ("It's OK to be angry but you cannot hurt your brother or his things"). Help her to channel her emotions positively by using words instead, such as "I'm very angry," or choosing other constructive outlets, such as pounding a pillow (or some clay), riding her bicycle (or other physical activity), drawing angry pictures, or dictating her feelings to you to write down. She will use these methods on her own to cope with her emotions as she grows.

Explain why he gives the younger one a hard time. You must also help him to see that when he constantly fires difficult questions at his sister and laughs at her answers or criticizes the way she holds her pencil, he is expressing hostility toward her and hurting her emotionally. You should talk to him about the underlying issue (sometimes he feels jealous and angry because it is hard to share your love) and talk with him about positive ways to express his emotions, such as coming to you and asking for a hug.

Teach her to stand up for herself. Encourage her to express her anger directly to her brother or anyone who is bothering her and teach her techniques in self-assertion, especially if she is fearful of standing up for herself. For example, you might suggest that she tell her brother, "I don't like it when you take my crayons without asking," or "I feel angry when I ask you nicely and you still won't leave my room." If someone took her ball in school and she comes home and tells you that she is upset, you can role-play with her or use stuffed animals or dolls to reenact the scenario. You can assume the role of the child who has wronged her and she can practice saying, "That's my ball. Give it back to me."

Act as a model. As parents, you must model constructive ways of dealing with anger in the family. You can talk about how annoyed you are at what Aunt Sally said and how you are going to call her and talk it over with her. If the two of you are having an argument, use positive communication techniques to express your individual needs and wishes. Ultimately, your children will mirror how you handle anger in the family.

Spend quality time with him. If your firstborn child is constantly provoking confrontations with you, observe his behavior and discuss the patterns with him. Create opportunities for positive inter-actions with him, such as taking him out for breakfast once a week. In this way, you will reassure him that he is loved and that he can connect with you in more positive ways.

Monitor your own behavior. Avoid automatically siding with your younger child, making comparisons between the two chil-dren, giving the oldest too many responsibilities, or pressuring her too hard, and she will feel less angry. Always be open to hearing what she considers to be unfair about her treatment.

Hold weekly family meetings. A family meeting at which every-one talks over the week's events can help all your children to express their feelings, clear the air, and get some needed reassur-ance. Set up a clear structure whereby you meet the same time every week—for example, Sundays between 5:30 and 6 P.M.—and you follow some mutually agreed-upon ground rules. Each person can speak for only three minutes (use a timer) using "I" state-ments, such as "I felt sad when . . ." or "I feel angry when . . ." and no one can hurt anyone else, physically or verbally.

Growing up as a firstborn child can be a very positive, enriching experience for children. Through their relationship with a younger sibling, they will learn a great deal about loving, nurturing, and pro-tecting another human being. They can also develop the capacity to be responsible, competent leaders.

If parents listen to them, are supportive of their feelings, teach them how to assert themselves, and try hard to treat them fairly in the family, they will grow up freer to benefit from their role as the older sibling and more capable of having a positive relationship with their younger sibling and with their parents.

3

The
Secondborn
Child

Four-year-old Michael sits wide-eyed on his father's shoulders, watching his seven-year-old sister, Rachel, take part in a swimming competition. The whistle blows; she jumps into the water, swims quickly to the other side of the pool, and wins the race!

Rachel is Michael's idol. It's been that way since he was a small baby sitting in his high chair, watching Rachel making funny faces at him. He adores her and thinks that she is the greatest. All day long, Michael shadows Rachel. He wants to be where she is and do what she's doing. If Rachel suddenly drops to the ground and does somersaults, Michael does them, too. If Rachel plays with Barbie dolls on her bed, Michael is sitting right beside her changing their outfits.

At dinner when Rachel says she wants chicken wings, Michael wants chicken wings. If she refuses carrots, he refuses carrots. When Rachel jumps up and announces she's finished eating, Michael is also done (even if he's still hungry). Parents often describe the way their younger child seems to merge into the older one. They find themselves working hard to remind their youngest child that he or she can make independent choices in life.

Rachel is Michael's first true love, and some of his happiest moments are spent playing with her. They have fun catching fireflies in a jar in the backyard, or cuddling up watching *The Wizard of Oz* together. Rachel is also Michael's first tutor. She reads to him, helps him to write his name on the chalkboard, and teaches him how to use the TV remote control. Rachel comes to Michael's defense when the neighborhood bully knocks him down. It is through his relationship with Rachel that Michael learns how to relate to peers—to share, to wait his turn, and to empathize with others.

Michael's relationship with Rachel is a mixed bag, however. Along with his closeness and affection for Rachel, Michael experiences feelings of inadequacy, jealousy and competitiveness, anger, rejection, and feelings of being left out or dominated in the relationship.

"I Can't Catch Up!"

🐛 *Michael is riding his tricycle along the sidewalk. Suddenly, Rachel whizzes by him on her two-wheeler. Michael pedals as fast as he can, but no matter how hard he tries, he can't catch up with her. He stops and watches her as she disappears down the street. Tears stream down his cheeks.*

It is hard for Michael to constantly contend with a verbal, physically stronger, more capable older sister. Rachel can ride a two-wheeler—he can't. She goes to school and can read and write—he can't. Rachel can chat endlessly with Mom and Dad about her day at school and family events. Michael can't get a word in edgewise.

As a result, Michael often ends up feeling very inadequate. He doesn't know that someday when he's older he'll be able to do many of the things that Rachel can do. Someday he, too, will be able to ride a two-wheeler. He will grow taller, his legs will be longer, and he'll reach the pedals. But, alas, Michael doesn't have that perspective. He just feels he's not as good as Rachel and he'll never catch up. When Mom and Dad get excited about Rachel's first report card—filled with Excellents and praise her for how smart she is—Michael gets worried: "If Rachel is so smart and she can do so many things that I can't, maybe I'm dumb—and maybe Mom and Dad love her more." In an attempt to stay on top, Rachel may enhance these anxieties by frequently criticizing what he says and does. Rachel's comments, such as "You can't even tie your shoelaces," or "You go to a baby school," add to his difficulties. In this way, Rachel keeps Michael in his place, to deter him from trying to catch up.

Effect on the Child's Development

Not only do these feelings of inadequacy cause him pain and anguish, but they shape his development. These emotions can be the beginning of a negative self-image ("I'm not as good as . . ." or "I'm not good enough . . .") that can affect him throughout life, academically, professionally, and in relationships. As a child, he may not try to hit a ball, run in a race, or do tricks on the monkey bars because he's afraid he won't do these things as well as Rachel. Or he may beat himself up when he makes a mistake. Even when he's doing great, he might not see it that way because he thinks Rachel is always doing better. In families where the older child is a "star" because she excels academically, or as a gymnast, pianist, or soccer player, the extreme focus on his or her abilities can enhance the younger child's anxieties. Such children may transfer these emotions to their peer relationships and feel inferior to their friends. Some younger children make sure to choose friends whom they can outshine so they can feel on top for a change.

Children's school problems often start here. Coupled with the fact that parents tend to make a big to-do when their firstborn child enters school, the younger child's fear that he can never measure up to his older sibling may interfere with his performance. For example, Michael may develop a math phobia because Rachel is so successful in this area and the family extols her for it. He may not even dare to try, or he may get overwhelmed with anxiety and therefore fail miserably. As a result of a snowball effect, Rachel may be labeled the "good student" in the family while Michael struggles throughout his school career—or, as we will see later in this chapter, he may become overly competitive to try to surpass Rachel.

Sometimes in an effort to differentiate themselves from a sibling, children search for their own areas in which to shine. Michael could become the "reader" or "artist" of the family. Though it's a natural thing to do, it remains sad that Michael has placed math off-limits. He may go through life convinced that he is unable to do math because he's not smart enough.

As adults, secondborn children often have no idea where their inadequacy feelings come from. Only through some self-analysis or with the help of a therapist are they able to see clearly that being the youngest in the family is one major source of the problem. Their birth order experience causes them to worry about their abilities and explains why they fear applying for law school, asking for a raise, or engaging in a competitive career. It even clarifies why they are intimidated by successful friends or still feel inept around their older sibling.

As we can see, it is urgent that Michael get help with these feelings early on because they can have lasting effects—and his parents can provide that help.

What Parents Can Do

Give your child emotional support. You can assist your secondborn child tremendously by being alert to this negative self-image; helping him to understand and talk about his feelings of inferiority; and showing an acceptance of his emotions. For example, if he is unhappy that he can't ride a two-wheeler like his sister, you can say, "We understand. You feel sad because your sister can ride a two-wheeler and you can't." You have labeled the emotion for him, and helped him to comprehend his inner world. By using the words "we understand," you have conveyed an acceptance of his feelings.

Help her to understand the reason why she feels inadequate. You might say, "It's hard to be the youngest child in the family. Your brother is older and can do more things than you can." Explain to her that all younger children worry when they can't do the things that their older sister or brother can. It makes them feel that they aren't as good and maybe Mommy and Daddy don't love them as much. But it's not true. Younger children will grow up and be able to do what the older children can do, and Mommy and Daddy have enough love for both of them. In this way, you have provided her with support and an emotional framework for understanding her experience. She feels the way she does because she is a second-born child.

Words are the best organizers of experience. When you tell a child that he is sad because his bird died, that it is natural to react that way when this happens, and that after a time he will feel better, the child relaxes. Anger, sadness, fear, or grief can be overwhelming to a child and make him physically and emotionally uncomfortable. Once the reason for these emotions is clear, he can organize himself to cope. Adults also benefit when they identify the source of their unhappiness. For example, realizing that the anniversary of a loss of a parent is approaching can clarify an undefinable depression and be a welcome relief. Once the younger child understands that there is nothing wrong with him that time can't heal and that he is loved no matter what, he will calm down.

Reassure the child that she is lovable. You need to reassure your child that she is lovable by saying, "Just because you can't do what your brother can do now, it doesn't mean that you never will be able to. When he was little he couldn't do more than you." Some parents find it helps to show their youngest child pictures of their older sibling when he was the same age. This reinforces that he was doing the same things and that their differences are only a function of age. Telling your children about your own personal experiences can also calm your child down. For example, you might say, "Do you know that I am a secondborn child like you? Now that Aunt Sally and I are all grown up, I can do the same things that she can. There are even some things that I can do better." Encourage her to talk to you when she feels upset. For example, you might suggest, "If you ever worry that you are not as good as your brother or that we love him more, come and tell us." This phrase encourages children to channel their feelings verbally. Always remind her, too, "In our minds, you are always as good as your brother and we have enough love for both of you." It makes children feel more secure. As you reassure your second child, she will internalize your words and use them to counter her insecure thoughts and soothe herself as she grows.

Praise him for his strengths and abilities. It is important to help your child see that there are things he *can* do and do *well*. Praise him for the way he sets the table, his sense of humor when he tells a story, and his ability to kick a soccer ball across a field. In this way he will learn that he is a valuable, capable person in his own right.

Involve her in activities at which she excels. As she grows, enroll her in programs where she can develop her special interests or talents and feel successful. For example, if she draws well or likes to paint, she can join a children's art class at a museum or an art school. She will see that she is a separate individual with her own unique abilities.

Avoid labeling or comparing your children. If your older child can keep her room neat, instead of labeling her the "neat" one, find ways to help the younger child learn to be neat too. Otherwise, some younger children, who initially had immature skills, may end up seeing themselves as disorganized throughout life. If the older child is doing well at school, be careful not to overpraise her in the presence of the younger one, for example by saying, "She's our genius." Reassure the younger one that when he is in school, he will do well, too.

Intervene when the older sibling puts the younger one down. If the older child puts down the younger one's ideas or abilities, you must stop him. You can say, "The rule is, you have to say kind things to each other." In this way, you are protecting your younger child, while giving her the message that you expect the same standard of her. When he criticizes her, she also needs to understand that she is not lacking but that her brother is having a problem. You can explain that sometimes it's hard for him to share the family's attention with her. He gets jealous and expresses his anger by devaluing her. Monitor your own behaviors, too. Your older child will emulate your approach to the younger one. If you innocently roll your eyes at the younger one when she buttons her shirt wrong and treat her as silly and incompetent, your older child will, too. Statements that are made in front of the younger one, such as "See! She doesn't even know how to get dressed. You're a big boy and you can do it!" to diminish the older one's jealousy, can upset the younger one, and therefore should be avoided.

Avoid babying the younger child. It is natural to baby the younger child in the family ("He's so cute!"). As much as the younger one and his parents might enjoy it at times, it can communicate that the child can't handle things or that he doesn't have to bother. Statements such as "Alex can't set the table, he's too little" or "Alex can't clean his room, he doesn't know how" can hold the younger one back. He might develop a lifelong pattern as a result of waiting for others to take over or take care of him (because he believes he can't possibly manage the task). When everyone is getting ready for dinner, it helps to give the younger one a job too, even if it's just carrying the spoons to the table. You should stop the older child from moving in to finish a task the younger one is having trouble completing. If he's trying to open a jar, wait until he asks for help. Everyone must give the younger child a chance to work through his difficulties. Whenever possible, ask for the youngest to make choices or to give his opinion about a subject.

All these methods will help your secondborn child to feel that "I can do things . . . I am lovable."

"You Love Big Sister More Than Me"

🐦 *It's 6:30 P.M. and Mom is sitting with Rachel helping her with her homework. After a few minutes, Michael inserts himself between Mom and Rachel, trying to show Mom a drawing he has made. Next he wants Mom to take him to the bathroom. When all else fails and the homework session continues, he kicks the cat. Eventually Mom and Rachel start yelling at Michael for interrupting them and he becomes the center of attention.*

All children feel jealous of their siblings at times. The basic issue that causes sibling rivalry is that children have to share their mother and father's love, and each child secretly or not so secretly wishes to be the most beloved child. This causes sisters and brothers to become hypervigilant to make sure that they are getting an equal share. When Dad pours the apple juice for the kids, all eyes are fixed steadily on their cups to see if the liquid reaches exactly the same level. At night the children watch to see whom Mom reads the bedtime story to first and how many minutes she spends sitting on each of their beds, and will protest if they feel cheated. Children are consumed with the questions "Is he getting more than me?" "Am I loved?" "Is she loved more than me?" Each child in the family wants to be loved the best. If someone else gets the extra drop of juice, two minutes more on the edge of the bed, or is read to first, it means Mom or Dad loves that one more.

Michael gets very jealous of Rachel when she shows off her new ballet steps at a family gathering and everyone applauds, or when Dad or Mom are going over her homework with her in the kitchen. In Michael's eyes, Rachel is getting more love and attention, to children time = attention = love (even if Mom is just testing her on her spelling words) and he can't tolerate it.

In essence, Michael has struggled with this issue since birth. Let's not forget that Michael entered the family in a very different way than Rachel. He never had his parents all to himself. And even though he had the advantage of being cared for by parents who were more relaxed and confident and could even enjoy him more, he had to share them with Rachel who was constantly trying to draw their attention away. And in many ways Rachel actually held on to the center of attention.

Once they brought Michael home, his second-time parents probably felt overwhelmed by the difficulty in balancing the needs of a crying baby and a demanding three-year-old who expected to have the same amount of attention as before. Because Rachel was omnipresent and interrupting them all the time, they probably found it hard to be alone with Michael. Like other parents, they may even have felt anxious about spending too much time with their new baby for fear of upsetting their older child, especially if she was acting up. As a result, they may have ended up handing over Michael to a relative or a baby-sitter, so that they could take Rachel out for a while and reassure her, or sneaking upstairs to grab a few moments alone with him while she was being entertained by some company in the living room.

In general, Michael fit into the preexisting rhythm of family life that was very focused on Rachel's needs. His daily life basically revolved around his sister's schedule. He would ride along in his stroller as they dropped her off at school, take his nap in the car seat on the way to her playdate, and crawl around on the sidelines at her baseball games. As Rachel told her parents stories about her day around the dinner table or sat and played board games with them, Michael was often the onlooker. But early on, he found all this focus upon Rachel to be unacceptable. He wanted attention, too. (Of course she viewed the situation from the opposite perspective.) In response, he naturally developed his own ways of inserting himself into the picture. He may have become the charmer, as many secondborns do, the cooperative one, if the older one was a problem, or the difficult child who ranted and raved. At four, Michael continues to get very jealous of Rachel because she still is often at center stage.

As the older child, Rachel is constantly involved in new firsts, such as starting ballet class or going on her first sleepover, which capture her parents' excitement and their attention. After all, this is the first time they have gone through this in the family. They spend lots of time driving her around to visit different dance schools, or shopping for the right sleeping bag for her in an effort to help her meet each new challenge in the best way possible. Rachel monopolizes her parents in other ways, too. She may chatter nonstop on the way to school, or absorb hours of their time working on a book report or talking about a problem she is having with a friend. And though Michael admires the wonderful new things his sister can do and is in awe about everything in her life, he feels nervous about all the attention she gets.

Not only that, but Rachel, who has been intent on maintaining her number one status since the beginning, has a hard time sharing the limelight. When Mom and Dad sit down to read Michael a story, she might immediately chime in: "Mommy, tie my shoe," or "I have a good idea. Let's play cards." Sometimes she'll even start a fight with her parents about taking a shower, to keep them focused on her. She might taunt her younger sibling, too. She'll tell him, "*My* mommy is picking me up from school tomorrow" and because of his age, he sees this as a serious threat. He'll retort, "She's my mommy, too," but Rachel will insist, "No, she's not."

But Michael struggles with jealous feelings over other issues, as well. He feels envious of the treatment Rachel gets as the oldest. She is always introduced first, is allowed to stay up later, and has the larger bedroom. He gets very upset because he sees that there are fewer pictures of him in the family album, when he gets Rachel's old baseball mitt while she has a brand-new one, and if the family makes less fuss over his birthday party than hers.

One of his deepest pains, however, is related to his awareness that Rachel had their parents all to herself for several years. When they are all looking at pictures of Rachel as a toddler, he might even deny this reality and announce, "I was just a baby then." It will be equally painful for him, too, to view the closeness between his older sister and their parents because she is the one they talk with and laugh with the most and will even take out to a restaurant and a show. His relatives may treat her as special, too. He does not realize that this has to do with their age differences. He believes they like her better.

Effect on the Child's Development

Michael's feelings of jealousy can be overwhelming. He may worry that Mom and Dad love Rachel more and don't really love him at all. Sadness and anger can be part of his daily experience. It may be hard for him to put his feelings into words, or he may be concerned that his emotions are not acceptable. Michael may act out his anger instead—for example, by distracting Mom every time she spends any time with Rachel. He may hit Rachel, break her things, not listen to Mom and Dad, and generally become a behavioral problem for the family. Michael may be the one at the dinner table who stands up on a chair to get attention. Many a younger child is labeled the "bad kid" or "problem child," and then a self-perpetuating negative cycle sets in. For example, when Michael misbehaves at the table, his parents miss what is really happening (he's jealous). They send him away, thus rejecting him for his outrageous behavior, and enhance his feelings of being unloved and his negative self-image (he is less lovable than Rachel or just not lovable at all). Feeling angrier, Michael needs to protest more, so he acts up even worse.

Michael's wish to be as loved or even more loved than Rachel can be expressed in other self-destructive ways. He may drive himself endlessly to compete with Rachel. If Rachel is doing five somersaults in the park, he'll try to do ten. He may transfer this competitiveness to his peer relationships, constantly trying to outdo others, and alienate his friends. If his best friend hits a home run, he may suffer emotionally because he feels inadequate.

Once he's in school, he may study all day long to top Rachel's grades, and as with many secondborns, his ambition may bring him great success. The danger here is that competitiveness will become a major part of his personality and he may evaluate his worth as a person according to his grade scores. He may set out to achieve, not for his own satisfaction, but to surpass Rachel. Even if he's very successful, chances are he'll never feel satisfied because he'll always be racing to catch up with Rachel in some new way. Michael may not engage in activities for his own pleasure but because Rachel chooses them. He will always seek to achieve some amorphous sense of being number one, granting himself little respite while always fearing that his older sister will be way ahead of him, no matter how hard he tries.

Adults often complain about driving themselves too hard, never knowing why. They'll talk about feeling empty when they achieve something—it is never good enough. These feelings may stem in part from being the second child in the family.

Some adults may react in an opposite fashion, however, and avoid competition entirely because they're convinced that they cannot equal their older sibling or because they may have felt undercut as a child by an angry sibling and, therefore, fear their competitor's wrath. As they go through life, they may avoid competitive situations, choose friends who don't threaten them, or avoid certain competitive careers. As adults, younger children will talk about getting tied up in knots whenever they must face a competitor.

Secondborns often suffer in their adult relationships because they are always comparing themselves to their friends and spouses and can feel crushed if they perceive that someone has more or is more successful (it makes them feel less valuable). They might even jeopardize important relationships by withdrawing or always trying to one-up the other. In short, their birth order experience affects their lives profoundly throughout adulthood. Early intervention from parents can make a significant difference.

What Parents Can Do

Convey that jealousy is acceptable. It is essential to convey that jealousy is natural, normal, and acceptable and that the family is a place where all feelings can be discussed and children will still be loved. Jealousy is often frowned upon in our society and deemed a negative emotion; everyone knows what Cain did to Abel. Children are taught that it is shameful to envy a sibling so they try hard to repress jealousy. Repressing emotions locks the pain inside and prevents children from getting help from their parents. For example, if your younger child is jealous because you are listening to his sister practice a new song on the piano, and decides this must be because you love her more, he hides the feeling because he is too ashamed to share such a negative thought. Then his anger and sadness build up inside, making him sad and depressed. It's preferable that he turn to you instead.

Talk openly about your child's emotion. When you sense that she is jealous, you can say, "We know it's hard for you to share Mom and Dad with your brother. All children feel jealous of their sisters and brothers at times because it's hard to share their parents' love and attention. But we have enough love for both of you." Tell her that you understand that it's hard for her to be the youngest child. Every night you sit for a long time with her brother going over his homework and can't be with her. In fact, her older brother is always doing new things and often needs your help. If she feels jealous, she should come and talk it over. In this way, you provide her with a forum for her feelings.

Reassure your child and help him to feel more comfortable. Emphasize that when you spend time with his sister it doesn't mean that you love her more or that you don't love him. Remind him that you spend time with him in other ways, building with Legos, flying a kite, and taking him for ice cream.

Together, search for solutions to help him feel better. Maybe if he wants homework too, you can give him some. Every evening he can sit next to his sister at the table, with his own notebook, feeling equally important.

In this way, he is reassured that he's not loved less and is given the opportunity to express his feelings. His feelings have been accepted and some solutions have been found to make him feel better. This certainly beats repression.

Help your child to express her feelings positively. When she is standing up on a chair at dinnertime to get attention, set a limit with her: "Standing on chairs is dangerous." Help her to understand why she's doing it—"We were talking with your brother and you wanted attention"—and encourage her to use words: "Next time tell us, 'I need some attention.' "

Intervene if your child is overly competitive. Learning how to compete is important for children. However, if you see that your secondborn child is driving himself too hard, or inflates himself at another's expense, talk this over with him. Reassure him that he does not have to outdo his older sibling or others to be loved. You love him as he is. He will need the same kind of support if he shies away from competition instead.

Involve your younger child in the older child's activities. When your older child is working on his science project, she can help him gather different-shaped leaves in the park. If he is in a dance recital, have her present him with the flowers at the end of the show. Her participation will help her to feel less jealous.

Make a big fuss over your younger one's events. If your second-born joins the soccer team, make it a big deal, even if your oldest child has been playing for years. When he has a special show at nursery school, invite your relatives. He will feel he is just as important as his older sibling.

Try to divide your time as evenly as possible. If you have spent an hour looking over catalogues for after-school programs with your older child, you might spend some extra time reading to your younger child or playing a game with her before she goes to sleep.

If your older child consumes your time by constantly fighting with you as his way of getting attention, try to diminish the battles so that your younger one is not neglected.

Avoid preferential treatment of any of your children. If your first-born is a star in some area, make sure to spread your praise, affection, and time equally between both children. Try not to stir up any competition between your children by comparing or labeling them, for example, by calling one of them your "cooperative child." If siblings are fighting, avoid siding immediately with "the baby." The younger one may have had a role in the quarrel and the older one will build up a great deal of resentment toward the family and her sibling if she is always blamed. The younger one will feel guilty, too.

Spend time alone with each of your children. Though it's often hard to find the time, or even to remember to do so, spending time with each child conveys that each is important, and brings you closer. A child who feels this connection will feel more comfortable and secure with sharing you. If you or Grandma and Grandpa take the older one to a movie and the younger one is too young to go, try to plan for a special outing for the younger one, too.

Set up external structures. Maintaining a running account of who sat in the front seat of the car the last time the family drove to the mall, or using a timer at bedtime to mark out an even amount of time spent reading to each child, are measures that will help children to relax about being loved equally.

Work with your older child. Help your older child to see that when he calls you away when you are reading to your younger child, tries to outdo her, or teases her, he is showing you that it is hard for him to share your attention. Suggest that he instead tell you when he feels this way.

Explain that things may not be exactly equal all the time. Children need to accept that sometimes another sibling will require more assistance or attention. For example, if one child is sick, the other child cannot be the center of attention. The younger one must understand that older children need less sleep so they can stay up later. He will have the same privileges as she does when he is older. A parent can communicate this while also acknowledging that these are very difficult concepts for children to accept.

When your secondborn child asks you why there are fewer pictures of him in the photo album, you can explain that it is harder for parents to take care of two small children than one. When he was born, they needed to use all their time to take care of him and his sister. Remind him that you take plenty of photos of him now. And when he complains that his sister had you all to herself before he was born, you might say, "We know that makes you sad. But it does not mean that we love your sister more."

"Play with Me!"

Michael and Rachel are playing Candyland in the den. Rachel's best friend, Emily, arrives and the two run off to her room. Michael follows, but when he gets there Rachel slams the door in his face.

Michael loves Rachel and wants to be with her. In the afternoon, he waits for her to come home from school, and when she arrives, he follows her everywhere. He wants to be in the kitchen with her when she has a snack, and in her room when she's doing her homework, or playing dress-up with her friends. Whether Rachel is reacting to Michael's constant crowding of her and a genuine need for space, is trying to be more separate and grown-up, or is still having trouble accepting his intrusion upon her life by being born—she ends up pushing him away.

Her shouts of "Go away!" or "Don't bother me!" ring out periodically throughout the day—when she's coloring in a coloring book and won't let him join in, when she's lying down watching her favorite television show and won't allow him to share the couch, or when she's swinging on a tire with her friends at the park and ignores him when he calls to her. She is rejecting him and he feels it.

In response to the rejection, Michael tries hard to get Rachel's attention. He walks around the house saying "cool" the way Rachel does, and even uses forbidden words such as "stupid" to make Rachel laugh, despite the fact that it makes Mom and Dad mad. When Rachel is fighting Mom about cleaning her room, Michael joins in and refuses too, hoping that Rachel will like him better for being on her side. He empties his piggybank of his last few coins and gives them to Rachel to buy stickers, if she asks, because he loves her and he is hoping for her affection. But still, Michael gets left standing on the wrong side of slammed doors, shut out and feeling miserable.

Sometimes, out of anger and frustration, Michael will provoke Rachel to get her attention. When she's watching her favorite show, he may switch the channel; he may knock over the checkerboard when she and her friend are playing or even hit her or call her names—negative attention is better than none.

Effect on the Child's Development

The feelings of rejection that Michael experiences can harm his self-esteem. If Rachel doesn't play with him, he may conclude that there must be something wrong with him. Maybe he's not likable.

As he grows, he may carry these feelings into other relationships and may worry that peers won't like him. He can be overly sensitive to a friend's momentary refusal to play blocks with him at school and conclude that the friend doesn't care anymore. When he's in the sandbox playing with two other kids, he may worry that he will be excluded, since this occurs with Rachel and her playmates.

In an effort to secure another's affection, he may adopt a friend's likes and dislikes and fail to explore his own. He may even repeat some of the negative attention-seeking behavior he employs with Rachel, such as starting fights with children at the playground when he really wants to be friends, because he fears rejection.

These relationship issues may follow him into adulthood and cause him problems. For example, his fear of rejection can prevent him from approaching someone he'd like to date. Michael might pick a fight with his wife to get attention when she's too busy with her friends or meld himself into a friend's identity to gain his favor.

It is important to note here that older siblings can often mirror how parents treat their children. So if Michael and Rachel's parents behave in a rejecting manner toward their children, Rachel might act that way, too, and intensify this outcome.

By dispelling the notion that Michael is being rejected because there's something wrong with him, his parents can prevent these powerful side effects.

What Parents Can Do

Explain why the older one rejects him. It is crucial that the younger sibling understand why the older one seems to push him away at times. He needs to hear over and over again that his sister is sometimes angry at him because she used to be the only child in the family and get all the attention and now she has to share the affection with him. This will help him to understand that he's not a worthless person, nor did he do anything bad to warrant her anger—initially, at least.

Help the younger child to give the older one privacy. The younger one also needs to see that because she loves her brother so much, she doesn't always give him enough space for himself and that also causes him to push her away. She can be taught that people need privacy, including time alone with friends. It doesn't mean her brother doesn't like her. You might point out the times she likes to dig in the sandbox all alone and gets annoyed when another child walks over. However, you can also encourage her to communicate with her brother about how she feels. For example, "Tell your brother that it makes you feel sad when he pushes you away."

Plan something special for your younger one. It is a good idea to invite a playmate for your younger child when his sister has one, so he won't feel rejected, or to plan a special activity to keep him occupied when she is unavailable.

Talk with your older child. Explain to your older child that he rejects his sister because he's mad at her. He used to be alone with Mom and Dad and now he has to share them. But his sister feels very hurt when he pushes her away and he needs to try harder. You will help him to have privacy when he needs it, but he must try to be kinder to her. For example, when he is busy, instead of yelling,

"Go away," he can say, "I need to finish my art project, but I will play with you later."

"It's My Turn!"

🐾 *Michael and Rachel are arguing in the living room. "I want to be the teacher," Michael screams. "Then I won't play with you," Rachel announces. Michael's meek "okay" signals one more time that he has given in.*

Whether it is because of her wish to be number one, her high energy level, or simply her size, Rachel usually dominates Michael in their interactions. If Michael wants to play Candyland, Rachel insists upon Chutes and Ladders. She must choose her piece first and make up all the rules, too. When they play house, Michael has to be the baby, even if he wishes to be the dad. Since she's more verbally astute and he hungers for her acceptance, she can easily manipulate him. She'll threaten not to play if he will not listen; bribe him ("If you let me watch my TV show, you can come to my birthday party"); and even trick him ("If you give me your new toy, you can watch my *Little Mermaid* tape when we get home," only to renege). And Michael usually yields. In this way, she constantly overrides his desires. Because she is quicker, she will grab the plate with a slightly larger piece of cake and be the first to plop down next to Mom on the couch. As a result Michael often feels frustrated and helpless to assert his wishes. Even though he's angry about this, he often bargains away his power in order to keep her involved.

Effect on the Child's Development

These interactions can strongly affect Michael's development. When Michael has a playdate, he may always yield to his friend's choices or relinquish his possessions too readily. He's convinced that he won't be able to get his way and that this is the way to keep the friendship. This behavior can ultimately leave him feeling unsatisfied and angry, since he can't fulfill his wishes. He can even end up being unsure of his own desires.

He may, however, react in an opposite way. He may become bossy with other children, because he is tired of being pushed around and is acting like Rachel, or become too possessive of his things. This behavior may push the other kids away.

As an adult he may continue to relinquish his desires, yielding to a boss's wish for him to stay late when he needs to leave, or accepting his wife's choice of a vacation spot that he won't enjoy. He may fear asserting his wishes because he'll incur the wrath of others or they will become uninterested in him. When given power, he may feel uncomfortable, because he didn't have much experience with being in charge as a child. Or if Michael becomes very bossy as an adult, he may alienate friends, family, and coworkers.

Of course, the parent-child relationship also greatly affects the child's development of self-assertion. If the parents allow Michael to express his opinion, make choices, and verbalize his anger, this will encourage him to stand up for himself. However, what happens with Rachel has a very powerful impact on how this ability will develop. If the parents are overbearing, this can strengthen Rachel's domineering behavior.

The ability to stand up for one's rights, advance one's ideas, and assume command are crucial for a person's happiness. Therefore, it is essential that parents monitor the sibling relationship, which becomes a model for how these issues will be handled in the future.

What Parents Can Do

Help him to understand why his older sibling is domineering. Explain to your younger child that sometimes his sister tries to be the boss when they play because she has trouble allowing him to be the center of attention. Just as she rejects him because of her wish to be the only child in the family again, she tries to overpower him, too.

Help the younger child to assert herself. When you see that she wants to choose the game and her older sibling is shooting her ideas down, intervene and support her. You can say, "Samantha wants to choose the game today. You need to take turns at picking a game to play." Encourage your younger child to speak up, too. She can tell her older sibling, "It's my turn" or "I'm playing with the ball now. You will have to wait."

Stop physical or verbal abuse immediately. If your older child is getting too rough with her younger sibling and he's mad, you should stop her and encourage him to tell her how he feels. (The same is true, of course, in the reverse.) If she puts his ideas or abilities down by saying, "You're stupid," when he's telling why he thinks it rains, or "That's not the way to do it" when he attempts to skate, she should be stopped. Tell her that no one in the family is allowed to call another family member names and that everyone's ideas are equally valuable. Explain that her brother is discussing his ideas or skating just fine for a child his age.

Engage children in problem solving. In an effort to teach children problem-solving skills, involve them in finding resolutions. You can say, "You are both playing school and you both want to be the teacher. What can you do?" If the children cannot come up with a solution, suggest that you set a timer and that they can each have a turn for fifteen minutes.

"What About Me?"

🐾 *It is the night of Rachel's play. Mommy and Daddy are busy helping Rachel put on her lion costume, finding their tickets, and calling their relatives to confirm the arrangements. Michael stands in the middle of the living room trying to tell the family about the new fish at nursery school while everyone rushes around him, too busy to notice.*

As the oldest, Rachel is frequently involved in a special event, such as acting in her first play, and her parents give her extra attention to carry it off successfully. But while this is going on, they are often unaware that they are forgetting about Michael or that he may have feelings about what's happening, and he can feel very left out. In other situations, such as conversations at the dinner table or a baseball game at the family picnic, Michael often ends up standing on the sidelines because his verbal and physical abilities are less mature, and he feels excluded.

In the scenario above, while everyone is rushing around and ignoring Michael, he may feel hurt and hide in the closet and wait to see if someone notices he's gone, or act out by throwing Rachel's costume on the floor. The family may mistake the message he is sending, thinking he's just being difficult, and get angry. But what his behavior is really saying is, "I feel left out. I need attention too!!"

Effect on the Child's Development

If Michael is always left standing on the side because everyone is too busy to pay attention to him, he may grow up having trouble relating to groups. At nursery school, he may withdraw during circle time when the group discusses the day's schedule because he's convinced that no one will pay attention to him if he tries to talk. Other younger siblings might react differently, however. They may thrust themselves into the center of the discussion and talk nonstop to try to keep the attention focused on themselves. They can have a hard time allowing other children to participate, or may drop back when the focus shifts away from them.

Younger siblings may have a hard time knowing how to join in when kids are playing in the playground, because of their concern about being ignored. This may continue into adult life. For example, as adults many younger children describe feeling like the outsider when socializing with a group of coworkers or even at home with their spouses and children. Some will characteristically not get involved in activities because they're sure no one is interested, and as a result they end up being ignored. Others won't relinquish the center of attention, and will alienate others.

Children need their parents to include them in events and to teach them how to be an active participant in a group.

What Parents Can Do

Explain why he feels left out. Help your younger child to understand that he feels left out because his older sister is often involved in something new or difficult that requires your attention. She needs help in learning her part in a play, or studying for her first math test. When he does these things, he'll get attention too.

You can also explain that when the family is talking at the table at dinnertime, she takes over because older children can think quicker and talk faster. As he grows, it will be easier for him to keep up. But when he feels left out, he should say, "I feel left out" or "I want attention," and you will help him to take part. He should also try to jump in when he has something to say.

Include your younger child. It's important to make room for each child in family discussions. You can suggest that each child say one thing in a conversation and then give the other child a chance. When you are busy with your older child, you might tell the younger one, "I really want to hear what you have to say, but you need to wait a few minutes." If your younger child is sitting quietly while everyone is chatting, you can ask, "What do you think?"

Have your child share in the responsibilities. If you and both children are doing something together, getting breakfast, perhaps, make sure that the youngest is sharing in the responsibilities. If she can't flip the pancake in the frying pan, she can help pour the bat-ter in. It's crucial that she feel included in some way.

Involve your younger child in a special event. If the older child is going away on a first sleepover, her younger brother can help her to pack her things, rather than standing on the side observ-ing the flurry of family activity. You might hold your younger child in your lap if you're watching the older one perform or, when the family is having a party, put him in charge of filling the pret-zel bowls.

Assign someone to watch over your younger one. When there is an upcoming event and you know that you will be distracted, try to assign someone, perhaps an aunt or uncle, to be her companion for the afternoon and give her special attention.

"You're Mean"

Michael and Rachel are sitting on the floor coloring. Rachel tells Michael, "I need the black marker," and pulls it out of his hand. In his fury, Michael starts throwing all the markers at his sister. Hearing the commotion, Mom enters the room and witnesses Michael's behavior.

Michael gets angry about Rachel's superior abilities, the attention she gets, her rejection and her domination of him. Since children don't come into the world with the ability to express their feelings verbally, they will resort to what comes instinctively: physical expression. When babies are mad because their bottle is not com-ing quickly enough, they cry and thrash about. Small children are not so far from babyhood, and so, when a young child is mad, he'll hit, kick, or throw something. This energy needs to be channeled into words. It is words that ultimately make people feel better. If you slam the door when you come home because you're angry at the boss, it may be a physical release of your tension, but it doesn't really help. Telling someone what happened, having them acknowledge and support your feelings, really makes the difference.

Michael, like all children, needs to learn from his parents the language with which to express feelings. In the coloring incident Michael feels overpowered by Rachel. A million times a day she has thrown her weight around: when he sat in his high chair, she used to sneak a furtive pinch as she ran by; while playing in the living room, she'd take away his favorite rattle when Mommy wasn't looking. All he could do when he was tiny was cry. Now, he is trying to assert himself but is getting very frustrated. He is no physical or verbal match for Rachel. So he seeks an alternate route to strike out at her, by throwing the markers at her.

A by-product of anger and jealousy is guilt. The younger child may wish that the older sibling would go away forever. Then the wish can make him feel bad about himself. Michael may also feel guilty if he successfully outshines Rachel, because he worries that she might be angry.

Effect on the Child's Development
Michael's unresolved anger toward Rachel can affect him powerfully as he grows. In situations where he feels put down, dominated, or rejected, he can become enraged. For example, he may knock down a block tower when other kids won't let him play. He may hit a child in the playground who won't let him have his way, or he may spit at his aunt when she tells him that he is writing his letters wrong. As an adult, he may become enraged if he feels that a boss is putting him down, his wife is trying to persuade him to do things her way, or his best friend is ignoring him. If he acts upon his anger by arguing inappropriately or distancing himself, he may lose important relationships or even jeopardize his career advancement. As a child, he needs his parents to help him to find ways to cope with his anger about his sibling relationship so that he can function more successfully in the world.

What Parents Can Do

Stop the negative behavior. In the anecdote above, when Mom walked in, she needed to set a limit on Michael's aggressive behavior. She could have said, "Stop! You can't hurt your sister"; stated the family rule, "We don't hurt anyone in our family"; and helped him to channel his feelings positively. "If you're angry, use words and we'll talk about it. You can say, 'I'm angry' or 'I don't like what you're doing.' "

Listen to each child's perspective. When an incident like this happens, try to piece together the events that led up to the negative behavior. Since there are two participants in any quarrel, they both typically have some responsibility—the child who transgresses first and the child who reacts. Ask both children to relate their view of the situation, to the other child say directly, "I feel angry when you take my things."

Talk about more appropriate solutions. If it was clear that the younger child was drawing and his sister had interfered, you could say to her, "You brother was drawing. If you wanted the black marker, you could have used another color or waited." And to him say, "If you needed the black marker, you could have said, 'I'm using it. You can have it when I'm done.' If your sister wouldn't listen, you could have come and asked the baby-sitter or Mommy and Daddy to help you."

Explain to the child why he feels the way he does. Later on, at a quiet moment, discuss the deeper issues with your secondborn. Tell him that you understand that it's hard for him to be the youngest child in the family. His sister is much stronger than him and can push him around. Talk over her deeper issues, too. At times she still feels angry about his intrusion in her life.

Teach him other ways to cope with anger. You might suggest that your child stamp her feet or hit a pillow when angered. Sometimes children enjoy acting out the anger through doll or puppet play, by drawing pictures, or dictating angry stories for you to write down.

Help your child with his guilt feelings. If your younger child expresses a wish that the older one would go away forever, you should communicate that he is not bad for having this wish. Convey to him that all children have these thoughts about their siblings, and explore why he is feeling this way. You should, however, emphasize that the older child is here to stay. It is very helpful for children to hear that there is room for two successful children in the family and that the success of one does not hurt or diminish the other.

Work with your older child. The older sibling has an agenda: to try to get the attention refocused on himself, the way it used to be, and this includes doing many things to keep his sibling out of the limelight. As we have seen he may engage in negative behavior, be verbally or physically abusive, attempt to dominate his sister, or leave her out. It's important that the family stop the older child from doing any of these things, and explain to him, in a loving way, why he is behaving this way. They can reassure him that the younger child can't take love away from him—there's enough for both of them.

Monitor your behavior. We have seen that parents can inadvertently add to the problems by leaving the younger child out, overemphasizing the feats of the older child, being unaware of what the younger child is communicating through his negative behavior, and getting mad at him when he's looking for more love. Parents need to be vigilant about birth order issues. Even the age-old tradition of always introducing the oldest first can feel oppressive to the younger child. Try reversing the order.

Growing up as a secondborn can be a wonderful experience for a child. There is an older brother or sister to look up to and to learn from. When things work well, the older sibling can provide companionship and nurture and protect the younger child. This relationship teaches the child how to relate to his or her peers.

However, aspects of this experience cause younger siblings much difficulty and can lead to serious problems as they grow. When the parent intervenes to explain the issues to the child, to lend support and teach some coping skills, the child becomes happier and freer to pursue his or her own interests and dreams.

4

The
Middleborn
Child

🌿 *Ten-year-old Rachel, seven-year-old Michael, and three-year-old Jenny are dressed up in scarves and hats, and are seated in a row on a blanket (their pretend magic carpet). They are acting out the story of Aladdin. Rachel is Jasmine, of course, Michael is Aladdin, and little Jenny is Abu, the monkey.*

Now that Michael is a middle child, he has two playmates instead of just one. Michael loves to play Monopoly, Battleship, and Nintendo games with Rachel. Though Rachel generally directs the play, she shows him how to do big kid things and he feels very grown-up. When Rachel is busy, unwilling to play, or is just being too difficult, he can spend time with Jenny. He gets a great deal of pleasure from playing school or action figures with her, and this time he can be the boss.

Though the children mostly play in pairs, sometimes they have lots of fun all together. When they are at the park or on vacation at the beach and no other children are around, they are each other's ready-made playmates. At times, the children can be very affectionate with one another. They will kiss "hello" and, when the mood strikes, even say, "I love you." They quickly band together against any outsider who dares to threaten one of them.

As a middle child, Michael is, in essence, both an older and a younger sibling, and he benefits from both of these positions. Growing up as a younger sibling, Michael has had the opportunity to observe and learn from his big sister. As a result, he was able to get on a two-wheeler and ride without instruction, and he began reading at an earlier age than Rachel.

Rachel will constantly spur Michael on to achieve as he grows. Michael will either model himself after his older sister, try to do better, or set out to be very different (become a spelling bee champion rather than a math whiz). He will also learn from watching Rachel's interactions with her parents which behaviors are acceptable in the family and how to get along successfully (Mommy and Daddy like it better when their children get good grades and keep their rooms clean).

Sometimes Rachel provides Michael with support and encouragement. She tells him, "You can do it," when he is afraid to jump into the pool, and "Good try," when he misses a ball. She also explains to Michael exactly what third grade will be like and what he needs to do to make the soccer team. At school and at day camp, he feels safer just knowing she is around.

Michael also gains from his role as an older sibling. Jenny idolizes him and shows him much love and affection. Each time he kisses Jenny on the head when she falls down or holds her hand as they walk down the street, he is learning to be a caretaker and nurturer. When he instructs her on how to button her shirt, watches her while Mommy is on the phone, or makes up stories for them to act out, he learns how to take responsibility and be a leader. This experience will build his self-confidence. He may, in fact, continue to be a source of emotional support for Jenny throughout life and extend this capacity to his family and other relationships.

As one of three children, Michael is naturally learning how to relate to a group: how to share, listen to others, and join in on activities. Because he has learned to deal with both an older and a younger sibling, each with a very different personality, and get his needs met through give and take, Michael will probably get along very well with others. Indeed, he may become particularly skilled as a negotiator.

Sometimes an oldest or youngest sibling will covet the middle child's position, declaring, "In my next life, I want to come back as a middle child." That is because the middle child is less pressured than the first, but is taken more seriously and is less overprotected than the youngest.

But the role of middle child has many difficult parts to it, too. Michael often feels left out, jealous, and very angry. He needs his parents to help him cope with these feelings so that he can grow up feeling loved and happy.

"I Need Attention!"

The family is sitting at the dinner table. Mommy is busy cutting up Jenny's chicken and vegetables. Daddy is having a discussion with Rachel about which language she might like to learn when she goes to junior high school. Michael suddenly flings a forkful of mashed potatoes across the table.

Before Jenny was born, Michael was the baby of the family. Mommy and Daddy used to bathe him and help him brush his teeth. They even carried him when he was too tired to walk home from the supermarket. Even though he often felt jealous of his older sister and fought hard with her to be the center of attention, he was comforted by his special place in the family.

But Jenny took away his role. Michael was no longer the adorable baby. Suddenly everyone was falling all over Jenny. The fact that she slept in Michael's old crib (in his room), ate in his old high chair, and sat in his beloved stroller was very difficult for him. Jenny has always needed so much of her parents' attention, too. Even at the age of three, she still takes away a great deal of time and attention from Michael, and to him, it often feels as if she is taking away their parents' love.

Michael's parents are often very tied up with Rachel, too. They are endlessly going over her lines with her for the school play, helping her fill out applications for sleep-away camps, or battling with her over whether or not she can wear makeup to her aunt's wedding.

Sometimes, Michael feels totally left out in the family. Mommy will be busy getting Jenny ready for bed, and Daddy will be in Rachel's room going over homework. Michael will call out for someone to come and read to him and, in response, receive a chorus of "wait a minute." He often ends up feeling very overlooked and unloved. At times, he will sit in a chair outside his younger sister's room or stand in the doorway of his older sister's room, waiting for someone.

Michael often experiences an identity confusion, too. He thinks to himself, "I'm not the oldest. I'm not the youngest. Who am I?" He wonders if somehow he is less special. There are fewer home videos of him than of Rachel, and he even wears some of Rachel's hand-me-downs. Mommy and Daddy are always smiling and laughing at Jenny's antics, but they get angry with him when he acts the same way. He often walks around feeling he is either too old or too young to be loved.

Michael desperately searches for ways to draw the attention to himself. Sometimes he makes his needs known, loud and clear: "I don't have enough time from Mommy," or "I'm always chasing after Daddy." At other times, he will inject himself into an activity. If Mommy is helping Jenny try on summer clothing, he will insist upon trying on his. Sometimes he will act silly, tell jokes to make everyone laugh, or chatter incessantly.

Some middle children become people pleasers to win affection. If Rachel asks Michael to put on her slippers for her, he might comply! He may be the first to clear off his plate after dinner, side with Mommy or Daddy against Rachel ("Mommy is right. You're too young to walk to the school yard alone"), and even tattle on Jenny ("Jenny pinched Rachel") in the hope of gaining favor. Other middle children will seek out close friendships as a way of getting the specialized attention that they are looking for. Some parents say that vying for attention is part of their middle child's personality.

Most middle children try hard to carve out their own unique identity so that they will feel special. While Michael's identity will be formed by many factors—his personality and talents, his relationships with his parents, and the family culture—it also will be sculpted around Rachel's identity. Michael will try to copy her, succeed in areas in which Rachel is having trouble, or search for arenas that can be his alone. Michael may become "Mr. Personality," or the cooperative one, sometimes in response to Rachel's more reserved or argumentative behaviors, and work hard to nurse his image along. If Michael were to receive positive attention for his artwork, he might draw night and day to perfect his abilities, especially if his older sister is not a successful artist.

To define himself, Michael could become obsessed with an interest such as baseball (and wallpaper his room with posters), or design a special outfit for himself (his trademark) that he insists upon wearing each day: an oversized tank top, a backward baseball cap, and baggy sweat pants. He will have a hard time parting with any piece of this attire on laundry day, because it is an integral part of his individuality.

At the same time that Michael is busily forging his own identity in relation to Rachel's, Jenny will be engaged in the same process with Michael. Trouble will begin for Michael if Jenny takes up Michael's passion for art, carries it to a higher plane by requesting art lessons, and ultimately ends up becoming a professional artist. Michael may feel angry because she has intruded upon his territory and taken away a piece of his identity.

To get their parents' attention, middle children will often resort to negative behaviors. Because they are having such a hard time, they can be a handful. Michael may provoke his older sister by barging in on her and her friends or throw his younger sister's teddy bear down the steps. He may have temper tantrums and scream at his parents, "You've ruined my life by having Jenny," or turn his room upside down. On the other hand, some middleborn children may give up and withdraw instead, especially if the parents are engaged in frequent battles with their older child or are overly involved in one of his sibling's activities. It is interesting to note that while he feels he is not getting enough attention, his parents may disagree. Because he acts up so much and they are trying so hard to include him, they may feel that they give him more attention than their other children.

Not only can a middle child feel a lack of attention from his parents, but he often faces rejection from his older sibling. Even though he keeps trying to get through to her, she will not give him an ounce of attention until she is ready. In part, this is because the older child has resented him since he was born and intruded upon her life. But as she grows, she is also naturally developing apart from him. At ten years old, her interests are changing. She would rather hang out with her friends and act cool than play catch with Michael.

Over the next few years, as Rachel develops physically and becomes interested in boys and dating, she will leave her brother far behind. At the same time, Michael's interests will change, too, and he will feel increasingly distant from his younger sister. The widening gap between him and his sisters will also be due to each child's involvement in gender-related pursuits.

Often the oldest child develops a stronger attachment to the youngest child than to the middle sibling. Because of the larger age difference, Jenny is less of a threat and more like Rachel's little baby. As a result, Rachel may take special pride and interest in Jenny. Since Rachel is probably more affectionate to Jenny than her more competitive, angrier older brother is, Jenny may naturally gravitate toward Rachel. She might prefer to crawl into bed and cuddle with Rachel in the morning, rather than with Michael. Because he is feeling left out, Michael may complain, "Before Jenny was born, Rachel loved me and took care of me because I was little. Now she doesn't love me."

As the three children grow, this triangle can become even more intense. Each time that Jenny and Rachel go off shopping or to the movies together without Michael, he might experience deep pain. Rachel may be unconsciously setting up this triangle because she is playing out her own feeling of being left out when Michael was born, by leaving him out. This may also be just another avenue for competing with him.

Effect on the Child's Development

If a middle child feels very left out and less loved than his siblings, he can grow up feeling anxious and insecure, and develop low self-esteem. As an adult, he may continue to experience a tremendous hunger for attention wherever he goes. He might sit in a roomful of people at a social, family, or work-related function, and be hyper-aware of whether others are paying attention to him. If as a child he tried to capture the center of attention by telling jokes or by entertaining others with funny stories, he may use the same strategies when grown. If he was accustomed to being left out and felt there was no use in trying, or found that being out of the spotlight was a safer position, he may remain quiet and just fade into the background.

Sometimes a middle child may find being ignored intolerable, however, and become explosive whenever he feels others are not listening to him. As he grows, he may run into trouble at school and in the workplace because he flies off the handle too easily. Reacting too strongly or totally withdrawing can leave the individual feeling even more isolated and unloved.

If as a child the middleborn gained favor by pleasing others, when he is an adult, he might quickly adopt others' opinions, change his viewpoints depending upon whom he is talking to, and even switch his loyalties to keep his bases covered. Because of his strong need for acceptance and love, or fear of confrontation, he might be afraid to say no and frequently find himself overcommitted. This behavior can backfire seriously. Rather than winning approval, he may make other people angry because they feel that they cannot rely upon him.

Like many middle children, Michael may find a distinct niche for himself in the family by becoming the peacemaker or "Mr. Fix-It." Being in the middle gives him a remarkable perspective on family relationships, and he may feel it is his obligation to fix everything. Everyone will turn to him when there is a problem and expect him to calm things down and negotiate solutions. Even though he might enjoy the sense of importance this role brings, he may end up feeling very overburdened.

If Michael has earned a different title, such as the responsible one, in the family, he may pressure himself relentlessly to live up to this identity; for example, he may insist upon being the one who always drives Mom to the doctor's even when it is not feasible. Unfortunately, living to please others or fulfill a family expectation can leave a person feeling out of touch with his own emotions (and wondering, "Am I a fake?"), feeling devalued ("What I want or think is not really important"), and angry ("Everybody's needs come before mine").

A middle child may gravitate to the performing arts because as an actor or a musician he can gain much recognition. This can be a very positive resolution for some individuals. Others may strike out against family norms as a way of establishing a unique identity, often when they feel that they cannot compete with their siblings. They may dress in a flamboyant fashion, choose a lifestyle opposed to that of the parents (decide not to go to college), and even become the "black sheep" of the family (hang out with the wrong crowd). Even when the path chosen brings only negative attention, he may feel pleased because at least he is being noticed. Unfortunately, some of these choices not only give him a sense of uniqueness, but they completely isolate him from the family. Sometimes realizing this will lead the child to identify with the family again later in life.

It is clear that feeling a lack of attention can affect the middle child's development and his sense of well-being. But parents can actively intervene to counteract the middle child's difficulties.

What Parents Can Do

Convey an understanding of him. You can help your middle child to feel more comfortable in the family by communicating to him that you understand him and that he is equally loved, and by giving him ample attention.

Address her feelings. You should help her to talk about any sadness or anger she feels about not being the baby anymore, reassure her that she is still loved, and emphasize that all children have a difficult time giving up this position. Let her know that you are aware of how hard it can be to be the middle child and share the attention with her siblings. You can explain to her that her younger brother needs a great deal of attention because he is young and cannot do very much for himself. When she was little, she received the same amount of care. And her older brother also gets a lot of attention because he is always doing new things that the family has never dealt with before, and he needs your help. You will support her in her new ventures in the same way, as she grows. But point out situations in which she gets attention when her siblings do not, such as when you work with her on a reading program on the computer or teach her how to play chess.

Reassure him. Above all, you must assure him that even when one child is getting extra time, you love all your children equally. Reading children's books with him about the middle child's experience, such as *Elisa in the Middle* (see bibliography), can stimulate a discussion with him about his emotions and help him see that he is not alone.

Encourage her to talk to you. It is essential to establish a clear line of communication with her, whereby she knows she can tell you when she is upset and you will listen and try to help. You should encourage her to use words to express herself, such as "I

feel left out" or "I need attention." If she can handle her feelings
this way, she will have less need to protest through negative
actions. Acknowledge her need ("I know it's hard for you to
wait"), engage her in joint problem solving when it is feasible ("I
have to watch your brother in the bath and you want me to read to
you. What should we do?"), or offer a suggestion ("Why don't you
finish the drawing you were working on, until I'm ready"). Sometimes talking through the evening schedule with her in advance—
for example, "First we will eat, then I'll give your brother his bath,
and then I will read to you"—will give her the assurance that her
needs are accounted for. All these measures can calm her down.

Help him to identify his negative attention-seeking behavior. At a
quiet moment, you should help him to see that when he kicks his
sister under the table, he is trying to get attention. But such behaviors only make everyone angry at him and he probably does not
feel more loved. It is better for him to discuss his emotions more
openly. When he tells you or his siblings how he feels instead of
acting out, praise him ("We like the way you are telling us how you
feel. Now we can help"). Positive reinforcement is often the best
antidote to negative behavior.

Pay attention to her. In general, the best way to help her feel
good in the family is to acknowledge her. When she mentions that
her teacher got angry at a classmate, relates that her brother said
she is stupid, or complains about a stomachache, try to stop what
you are doing, tune in to her, and show interest and support (e.g.,
"Tell me about it" or "Show me where it hurts"). When the family
is sitting around and talking at the dinner table, seek out her opinions and ideas. She will feel important and loved.

Spend time with him. You must also monitor the amount of time
that you spend with your children, to make sure that the middle
child does not fall through the cracks. Like his siblings, he needs to

spend time alone with you, too. Though juggling the needs of three children or more is not an easy task (getting help from a spouse, a friend, a relative, or a sitter to get through the roughest times of day is best), most parents find that when they give their middle child some special one-to-one attention, it makes a huge difference. Spending some extra time with him during the day playing his favorite card game, or setting up a specific outing with him each week, can make him happier. When you are busy, try to include him in his siblings' activities.

Encourage the older child to include her. Your older child should be encouraged to spend some time with his sister and to be sensitive to her feelings. Intervene when he openly rejects her and help him see that when he pushes her away (or constantly chooses to play with his brother and not her), he makes her feel very bad. Ask him to include her more and handle things in a more sensitive, respectful way. For example, he can tell her, "I need to finish what I am doing, and then we can play checkers." At the same time, you should insist that she respect her brother's privacy and avoid teasing or provoking him. Otherwise, she is setting herself up to be rejected.

Explain why his older sibling rejects him. You should also clarify for him that his older sister pushes him away because she is very angry that he was born right after her and took away her place as the baby in the family. Perhaps he pushes his little sister away for the same reason. Reassure him that there is nothing wrong with him, and that he did not do anything wrong.

Help her build a positive identity. Support her in her struggle to develop her own identity. When you ask her opinions about where the family should have a picnic, which shirt she would like to buy, or how she feels about her friend moving away, you will help her to be in tune with her emotions and develop a strong sense of self. You should also be attuned to her interests and talents and find ways to encourage her. For example, if she seems to have a gift for computers, you might enroll her in a special computer program.

If your middle child's identity is too tied to pleasing her older brother or others, help her to assert herself and draw some boundaries ("It is nice that you want to help your friend, but you can tell him that you will come over after you do your homework"). You should intervene to stop her brother when he manipulates her with such demands as "If you want to come to my birthday party, you have to make my bed."

When she puts together a funny-looking outfit to wear to school or decides that she loves heavy metal music, do not make fun of her. Try to be as flexible as possible so that she will feel respected, and set limits with her instead. For example, she cannot wear this outfit to a family party, or she can listen to her favorite tapes only behind closed doors or with headphones.

As she gets older, if her expression of individuality becomes extreme, such as dyeing her hair purple, it will usually be a sign that she is crying out for attention. This type of acting-out behavior often has to do with the child's feeling of isolation from her parents. In such a situation, you would need to set stronger limits (she cannot change the color of his hair) while working hard to build better communication with her. You need to elicit her feelings, and listen to her noncritically, while conveying love and acceptance. Family therapy might be very beneficial in such situations; it can provide the family with an arena in which members could receive needed support and guidance to build stronger relationships.

"You Like Them Better than Me"

🐦 *In their aunt's wedding party, little Jenny is going to be the flower girl. Rachel is going to walk down the aisle as a junior bridesmaid. But Michael, who is at an in-between age, has not been given a part.*

Michael feels very jealous of his two sisters. Each one is constantly doing something that brings her into the limelight. It is Rachel who takes the whole family on new adventures all the time. There is constant talk at the dinner table and in the car about her starring role in the school play or her first time at sleep-away camp. Grandma and Grandpa and her aunts and uncles call up to hear the latest and feel excited for her, too. With her high grades in school, her talent in gymnastics, and her beautiful blue eyes, everyone says she is a hard act to follow.

Friends and relatives pay close attention to Jenny's growth, too. After all, she is the baby and perhaps their last child. She is so adorable and sweet. The family is interested in how she is doing at nursery school and what funny things she has said recently.

Somehow, Rachel's and Jenny's advances seem to be more dramatic than Michael's. There is less of a fuss at almost anything Michael does, whether it is starting to read or joining Little League. Everyone has been there only a short time before with Rachel. Because he's no longer an adorable preschooler and, at his age, has not as yet shown his true abilities, he can be easily overlooked. (However, since he is the only boy, people may pay him more attention.) Michael's parents often intensify his jealousy by adopting pet names for Jenny, such as "princess," or describing Rachel as "our math whiz." He frequently worries that he is not as special as his sisters and that they are more loved than he is.

In the chapter on the secondborn sibling, we saw that as a secondborn child, Michael often feels inadequate, because Rachel can do so much more than he can. He does not realize that the reason Rachel is more skilled is that she is older and that children's abilities improve as they grow.

He works hard to equal his sister. He copies whatever she does and tries to do it better. But often his feelings of inadequacy get in the way. When the family takes him skiing for the first time, he may don the skis and quickly learn the maneuvers. But as soon as he sees Rachel going up on the ski lift to a more advanced hill and he cannot go, he might decide that he is not as good as she is and remove his skis. Though initially he may feel glad that he has finally learned to read, he might feel insecure because he cannot read at Rachel's level, and even refuse to do his evening reading assignment. His frustrated parents may have no idea why.

Not only does Michael feel inadequate because he views Rachel as so much more capable, but Rachel, in her own ways, adds to this feeling. She constantly taunts him ("You only have one excellent on your report card; I have five").

Having a younger sibling who idolizes him as much as Jenny does can help. He is the competent older brother. He can hit a ball with a bat and do cartwheels; she cannot. While this might make him feel a little better about himself, he is so focused on his rivalry with Rachel that he may not value his superiority over Jenny as much.

But Michael also feels very competitive with Jenny. He feels jealous that she gets so much attention. He does not understand that young children naturally require more care than older children or that grown-ups tend to gravitate toward adorable younger children and enjoy watching them develop. He may feel that being his age makes him less valuable. Sometimes he will regress and try to act like Jenny so that he will be noticed. He might use baby talk or refuse to dress himself. Rather than winning him more affection, this behavior tends to drive his parents crazy!

While Michael is trying hard to keep up with Rachel, he is often panicky because Jenny is frequently closing in on him from behind. On a family fishing expedition, he may be intent upon catching a fish before Rachel and feel very upset when Jenny upstages him by catching the first fish. In the same way that Rachel uses putdowns to stay ahead of Michael, he uses the same tactics with Jenny. He will tell her, "You're casting all wrong," in an effort to communicate to her that she is inferior and undermine her progress. Of course, he also resorts to this behavior because he feels so targeted by Rachel and inferior to her.

Michael's jealousy and competitiveness is so intense that he insists on having the same exact birthday party that Rachel had and he may become enraged if he sees Mommy taking Jenny's temperature when she feels sick because she did not take his when he was not feeling well. The minute he feels slighted, he may scream, "You love my sisters more than me." (Of course, they may believe that he is the most favored one.)

Effect on the Child's Development

Life is definitely harder for Michael as a middle child than it was as only the secondborn in the family. He now has two contenders. He constantly looks above him and below him in the birth order and feels a need to compete to be loved.

Competitiveness may end up becoming a major part of his personality. He will drive himself hard to catch up with or surpass Rachel, while rushing to keep ahead of Jenny. He will try to be the best student, a superior athlete, and the most popular kid. As he grows, he may try to outdo his siblings by earning a larger salary, living in a bigger house, or having the first grandchild. He will play out this competitiveness with his friends, coworkers, and even his spouse. Unfortunately, he may suffer emotionally and physically from internal pressure, or feel bad about himself whenever he feels he is not at the top—the same way he may have felt when he was placed in the second best class at school.

On the other hand, if he grew up convinced that he could never equal his siblings, he might avoid competition entirely, or pull back the moment he faces tough competition, especially from two rivals. For example, when a colleague is made a partner in his advertising firm, he may drive himself hard to catch up. But as soon as a young upstart in the company starts moving up through the ranks and threatens Michael's advancement, he may find it hard to produce. Unconsciously viewing his coworkers as his more victorious siblings of the past, he may become fearful of defeat and drop out of the race altogether. Because of an underlying feeling of inadequacy, a fear of failure or a fear of success, like other middle children, he may develop a lifelong pattern of starting something and then not persevering.

Being successful may also raise other complicated issues for Michael. He may go through life continuously conflicted about success because he feels guilty whenever he has more than his siblings. When he is about to make a purchase, he may torment himself: "How can I have a new car when they do not?"—especially if the older one drives an old beat-up jalopy, or the younger one needs a car to get to her classes. He may feel frightened that Rachel will become angry because she usually gets jealous, or that he may have to chauffeur Jenny around because he feels so obligated to take care of her.

Feelings of jealousy and a constant need to compete can end up causing Michael tremendous pain, interfere with his relationships, and diminish his chances of achieving his goals. If his parents are aware of his struggles and handle situations carefully when he is a child, he will grow up feeling more self-confident and freer to build a successful life.

What Parents Can Do

Be accepting of his feelings. As with all your children, you must be accepting of your middle child's feelings of jealousy. When he complains that his sisters get more love and attention, listen carefully to what he is saying. If you dismiss his feelings or make him feel guilty, he might see his feelings as bad and repress them. When he says, "You love my sisters more than me," you can ask, "What makes you feel that way?" He might see the fact that you greeted his sisters before him when you came home from work as a sign that this is true. (This may even happen every night because his older sister easily outruns him and his little sister outwhines him.)

Offer her reassurance. Reassure her that even if one child gets a little more at one moment, all of them will receive enough love.

Some parents find that it calms their children down if they set up concrete rules about certain situations. For example, each night when you arrive home from work you will kiss a different child hello first.

Be alert to his feelings of being loved less than his siblings. As you should with any younger child, be alert to any sign that he feels inadequate in relation to his older sister. If, for example, you discover that he has hidden his report card from you, consider the possibility that he did this because he believes that his sister got a better one. She may have even teased him about it. Help him talk about his anxieties about not equaling his sister and explain the objective reality to him: she can do more because she is older.

When he is feeling jealous because his little sister is counting to ten for the family and everyone is sitting spellbound listening to her, help him with his feelings. Inform him that people are naturally drawn to little children, so they give them a lot of attention. Remind him that when he was small, everyone was enraptured when he started counting, too.

Encourage your family to give all your children equal attention. In general, parents should make sure to keep their relatives informed about all of their children's progress, so that each one will receive ample attention. Some parents even send out a family newsletter from time to time. When there is a family gathering, be careful not to set up a situation in which everyone is focused on only one child.

Promote positive interactions among the children. It is important to monitor how the children interact and intervene if one criticizes or disparages another in any way. It is essential also to avoid comparisons of your children, especially complimenting one to the detriment of another. If you make a statement such as "Becky and Lauren are so cooperative," your middleborn will feel that she is the bad one in the family. Her sisters will feel guilty because they are being elevated at their sibling's expense.

Help him feel loved and confident. The best way to help the middle child feel less jealous and more secure in the family is to show him that he is special. A touch, a smile, a hug will convey to him that he is adored; so will spending time alone with him reading him his favorite book. When you tell him, "You are our special seven-year-old," "You look so cute with your new haircut," or "We love you," he will know you care.

Praise him often. Tell him, "That was a good suggestion" (he is smart), "We like the way you shared your muffin with your sister" (he is a good person), "You did a great job fixing your bike" (he is capable), "We had such a good time with you at the ballgame" (he is likable), and he will see himself in these positive terms. He will like himself, feel confident about your love, and worry less about your affection toward his siblings.

"I Hate You"

🐦 *Michael knocks on Rachel's door. From inside, Rachel yells, "You can't come in. My friends are here and you're not cool." Michael storms into his room and kicks Jenny out, shouting, "No babies allowed!"*

As we have seen, Michael feels angry about losing his role as the baby in the family, especially when he thinks he is not getting enough attention. But he also becomes enraged when he senses that his siblings are being treated better than he is, when his sisters give him a hard time, and when he is unable to assert his wishes.

Michael is resentful that Rachel has many special privileges that he does not. Rachel can stay up at night an extra half hour and is allowed to go to movies that he is too young to see. She can walk to the store all by herself, but he has to have a parent or Rachel accompany him. Because she is older, Rachel gets to do everything first.

Michael feels shortchanged about other things, too. His whole day seems to be organized around Rachel's activities. He is constantly dragged from Rachel's gymnastics practices to her after-school programs to her birthday parties. Rachel has a room all to herself, while he has to share one with Jenny. He may be begging for piano lessons, but because Rachel never practices his parents are reluctant to let Michael start. When Michael was younger, he used to watch all of Rachel's baseball games with Mommy and Daddy. Now that he has finally joined his own team, Mommy often ends up staying at home with Jenny for one reason or another, and Daddy can only watch half his game because he has to watch Rachel's, too.

In his view, his parents also seem to have different rules for Jenny and him. When Mommy and Daddy are talking, he is told that he cannot interrupt. He must wait till they finish. But if Jenny starts whining, they will stop and answer her or give her exactly what she wants. She always seems to get her way, too. If she wants to hold his new Batman figure and he does not want to give it to her, Mommy or Daddy might say, "Just let her have it already." He does not realize that they are only trying to quiet Jenny down.

He is enraged that Mommy constantly asks him to keep an eye on his sister, that the baby-sitter treats Jenny like a baby (she sits and rocks her all the time), and that Daddy blames Michael for all of his arguments with Jenny. To add insult to injury, Jenny has a pair of Rollerblades already, and he did not get his first pair until he was five.

Though he has many good moments with Rachel, Michael can become infuriated by the way she treats him. He hates the way she bosses him around all the time. When they play board games together, she insists upon making up the rules, only to change them as soon as she starts to lose. Michael can't stand being manipulated by his older sister either. She will promise that if he allows her to use his bicycle when hers has a flat tire, he can use hers the next day—then usually she reneges. Even though he gets frustrated with her, he often puts up with her behavior because he idolizes her and wants her attention so badly.

Dealing with Jenny is not exactly a picnic for Michael, either. He generally finds her to be an intrusion in his life, especially because the two share a room. He is very disturbed by the way she follows him around all the time, copies him, and messes up his things, and he will often overreact to her. Sometimes he will have a tantrum the moment she comes near.

But Michael has a hard time dealing with his rage toward either sibling. Rachel is bigger and stronger than he is, and when they fight she quickly pins him down. In a war of words, she can easily find a more cutting remark to make. As a result, he tries hard to negotiate with her, but he knows when it is wise to back off.

Expressing anger toward Jenny has its own complications. Since she was born, Jenny has been poking Michael, pulling his hair, and breaking his toys. But he has been warned that he must not retaliate against her or harm her in any way. If he does, he is yelled at or punished.

The need to be mindful of the limits with both his siblings causes Michael to hold in his anger at times, and he can end up feeling very frustrated and defeated. Or he will find subtle ways to get back at his siblings. He will tease Rachel by telling her friends that she has a crush on a certain boy, or will use his older sibling power to dominate, reject, and criticize Jenny not unlike the way Rachel acts with him. In fact, when Rachel treats Michael badly, he will commonly take out his frustration on little Jenny.

As we can see, Michael is often exasperated by both his siblings and he struggles hard between his wish to retaliate and his fear of risking Rachel's or his parents' wrath. Controlling his emotions, therefore, is a major challenge for him.

Effect on the Child's Development

Like many middle children, Michael may grow up feeling very angry. Sometimes he will feel so upset with his parents and his siblings that he just loses control and screams, tears up his room, or hurts his sisters, especially if these have become proven methods for getting attention. If he frequently behaves like this, Michael might become such a handful for the family that he is labeled the "bad child." Unfortunately, he may then grow up viewing himself as bad, too. His parents can exert tremendous energy talking to him or screaming at him and punishing him, but because he is so unhappy, he may be unable to stop his behavior. They may end up feeling very furious and defeated. Sensing his parents' dissatisfaction with him, Michael may worry that he is not loved at all.

If the situation is not remedied early on, Michael's anger and aggression may spill out into his school life, where he might be aggressive with the other children, or engage in disruptive, negative attention-seeking behaviors. If his relationships with his siblings and parents continue to be very combative as he grows, he may end up distancing himself from the family. Later on in life, his powerful rage reactions can interfere tremendously with his success in the work environment and with important relationships.

Michael may develop a coping mechanism of repressing his anger instead, or he might alternate between acting out and holding his feelings in. This may happen in part because he is very afraid of arousing Rachel's anger. He has had enough experience as Rachel's younger brother to know that if he refuses to do what she wants or tries to fight her, she will retaliate tenfold.

But Michael may also be afraid of his own anger. Sometimes his emotions may seem so big that he worries he could really hurt his siblings, especially Jenny. Even his hostile thoughts can make him feel guilty. In his experience as Jenny's older brother, he knows that any aggressive act he takes toward her could lead to serious consequences. If his parents reproach him in a harsh, punitive fashion or are generally unaccepting of his feelings, his anxiety about expressing anger will be heightened.

But Michael may sit on his anger for another reason as well. If Rachel constantly fights with their parents, Michael will learn that it is safer not to do so. In order to be acceptable and valued by his parents, he will do the opposite—he will act quiet and compliant.

If he receives positive acclaim for not showing his feelings, this pattern of handling anger will become entrenched. It will also be detrimental to him if his parents label him their "good" child because he does not have a temper like Rachel's. Despite any momentary pleasure he receives from this special recognition, he will ultimately end up experiencing guilt toward his sibling.

Avoidance of anger can have a disastrous effect upon Michael's emotional well-being and his relationships with others. He may grow up fearful of asserting himself and arousing other people's anger. As a result, he may spend his life trying to appease others and running from confrontations, never really feeling safe in relationships or capable of solving problems. Some adults unconsciously turn their anger against themselves instead. They blame themselves for everything. It may feel safer; they can protect the other person, and no one will harm them.

Michael may even fear acknowledging his own emotions to himself—his aggression may seem too terrible—and he might end up feeling cut off from his emotions. If he never confronts his anger or expresses his feelings openly, he will probably feel very anxious because of the energy needed to push down his emotions, and he may remain emotionally distant from those he loves.

It is important to note that specific experiences Michael has had as a child, in his dual role as an older sibling and a younger sibling, will affect the way he perceives and reacts to situations as an adult. For example, because he has felt so intruded upon by Jenny, when he is a parent he may reexperience similar rage when he finds his child rummaging through his drawers to find the Scotch tape or using his computer without asking. Because he was so angry that Jenny was overly protected by their parents, he might blow up if he gets blamed by his boss for a colleague's mistakes.

Sparked by his unresolved anger toward Rachel for her mistreatment of him, Michael might fly off the handle when someone kids around with him in a mildly sarcastic fashion, or when his wife tries to make choices for him in a restaurant. When he is enraged, making these connections to his childhood experiences will help him to put the situation into better perspective, and he will be able to react more appropriately. Because Michael has grown up as both an older and a younger sibling, he may be forceful at times and passive at others, depending upon whom he is dealing with. For example, he may be overly domineering with his children, but back down too quickly when relating to an older coworker.

As the middle child, Michael desperately needs help from his parents to find positive outlets for his emotions so that he will feel happier in the family and will be able to build satisfying relationships.

What Parents Can Do

Address his anger directly. Direct communication is the key. The middle child will feel less alone and act out less if he knows his parents will listen, accept his feelings, and provide him with support and love. They will, in essence, be acting as his allies.

When it is clear that he is throwing his toys around because he is angry, you can respond, "It is OK to be angry, but throwing your toys around is not acceptable. You need to use your words. Say, 'I'm angry.' " Then, try to uncover the cause. You might ask him, "Did someone do something that made you mad?" It is easier for young children to answer this question than one such as "What's bothering you?" When he is too angry to speak, you might suggest that he use his punching bag or write his feelings down and then find a quiet moment to talk with him about what happened. If you know what event precipitated this reaction, you might say, "I went to the theater with your sister. You probably felt left out and angry that she gets to do some things that you can't do yet. But it's best to talk about your feelings, so we can help you."

Clarify for her why her older brother is often given more privileges than she is. Explain to her that he can stay up later because he is older and he needs less sleep than she does. He can go to the store on his own because he is able to cross the street by himself.

At her age, he did not have these privileges, either. When she is older, she will have the same opportunities.

Give him some firsts. It would probably make him feel a whole lot better if he were to have some firsts before she did. For example, he might be offered the chance to go to Disney World with his grandparents even though his sister has never gone with them. Also make sure that he has plenty of his own activities, and participate with him when he does, even if it means hiring a baby-sitter for your youngest from time to time. It is important that you celebrate with him when he gets his first baseball trophy, even if his sister already has three sitting on her shelf.

Listen and explain. When your middle child complains that she never gets attention, don't try to immediately talk her out of her feelings. Parents often find it hard to listen to such complaints because it makes them feel that they have been remiss as parents. Instead, listen carefully to the way she sees things. Her complaint may have some justification. For example, if she says, "You always bring Chloe into bed with you in the morning, but I'm not allowed," you might explain, "That's because she is little. She cannot play on her own as well as you can and we want to sleep a little longer." If you reassure her that she was treated the same way when she was small (she probably does not remember) and that when her sister is her age she will have to behave just like her, she will be comforted. If you point out that she is allowed to go on sleepovers and her sister cannot, she will see that she gets special privileges too.

When she protests that Chloe got Rollerblades at a much younger age than she did, you can remind her that you bought her a two-wheeler at an earlier age than her older brother. Besides, parents often allow their younger children to try new things at an earlier age because they have already been through the experience with another child, and thus feel more comfortable.

Try to treat your children as equitably as possible. To diminish your middle child's resentment toward his younger sibling, try to include her in cleaning up the toys, along with her brother. If she is acting up and bothering her brother, hearing you set a limit on her behavior, such as "Pinching your brother is not allowed. We don't hurt anyone in our family," will give him the feeling that he is supported. You should avoid asking him to watch her all the time, too. He will feel less put upon. When the two children are fighting, be careful not to immediately scold and take the little one's side. Otherwise, he will believe that you love her more. Instead, address both children: "Roughhousing can lead to someone getting hurt."

Explain her younger sibling's behavior. Help your child to comprehend that little children have a hard time controlling themselves—that is why her brother interrupts them all the time. You are slowly teaching him how to wait. Hopefully, with this understanding, she will be able to adopt a more instructive approach with him at times, and flare up at him less. Not only must you treat her fairly, but you should emphasize the importance of this with the baby-sitter (who may be more attached to the baby) and your relatives, too.

Raising the middle child's consciousness about the similarities between her relationship with each of her siblings can help her to understand herself and accept the little one more. You can explain that her younger brother wants to be with her all the time for the same reason that she wants to be with her older brother. He loves her and thinks she is the greatest. When she rejects him, he feels just as sad as she does when she is rejected. So she must treat him carefully.

Help him to have privacy. Safeguarding his privacy will also help him to feel less resentful. Acknowledge his need and help him to have some time alone. Tell his little sister that he needs privacy, keep her busy with other activities (so that he can have his room to himself for a while), or have a playdate for her when he has a friend over. He should not be forced to share his toys with her. She must ask him for something, but he can say no, especially when it is a new toy or a valued possession. He should be encouraged to keep his special items in a safe place, and store his most prized constructions high up on a shelf.

For some middle children, the issue of the older one having a room all to herself while he has to share can be a big one. The middle child can be very angry and take it out on the youngest child and the family may not have a moment of peace. Some parents try to remedy the situation by converting a breakfast nook into a third bedroom, or finding some way to divide the joint bedroom into two rooms. If this is impossible, the middle child will need lots of support.

Intervene when her older sibling is domineering. You can help ease her difficulties with her older sibling by intervening when he is bossing her around, hitting her, manipulating her, or calling her names. You might reinforce her desires ("It's your sister's turn to be first today"), or set limits on his behavior ("Calling people names or hitting anyone is not acceptable in our family"). When he pushes her out of the living room where he is watching TV with his friend, restate the rule: "When you have a friend over and you watch TV with him in the living room, your sister has to be included. When you're in your room, you can be alone."

Listen to his requests. When he asks to take piano lessons or to go to sleep-away camp like she does, weigh his requests carefully, rather than immediately declaring that he is too young. Otherwise, he will feel terribly slighted. Besides, he may actually be ready. Let him make his case, discuss the issues with him, and only then decide (of course, it is ultimately your decision). He may even come to some conclusions on his own—he is prepared to take on the responsibility of learning music but he is not ready to go away from home for a month.

Teach her how to assert herself. She should be encouraged to stand up to her brothers when they are bothering her. Suggest that she tell her older brother, "You cannot change the rules once we make them," or her little brother, "You have to ask me if you want to use my coloring book" (and when she does, praise her). You can play out different scenarios with her using puppets or dolls to help her practice self-assertion. You should instruct her that when one of her brothers is bothering her, she can also call an adult for help, walk away, or choose to play with her other sibling. In this way, you are teaching her important social skills that she can use in all her relationships. If parents communicate positively with one another and with their children, they will serve as excellent role models, too.

Middleborn children's position in the family can be a difficult one, but if parents work hard to help them feel included, convey that they are special, and help them to find effective ways to deal with their feelings, they can benefit tremendously from the positives of their position.

5

Twins

It's the Sadie and Dora show," seven-year-old Sadie announces. *Dora, her fraternal twin, leaps into the living room and twirls around on her toes, while Sadie sits cross-legged on the floor, strumming on her guitar.*

There are two kinds of twins: identical twins, formed from one fertilized egg; and fraternal twins, formed from two fertilized eggs. Identical twins, always of the same gender, look exactly alike or are each other's mirror image. Fraternal twins can be of the same or opposite sex and their similarities vary. However, there is a common thread for all twins: two children born only moments apart are growing up together.

Sadie and Dora share the same room, toys, friends, classes, and even their birthdays. This situation creates a unique bond between them. Because they spend so much time together, they feel close and comfortable with each other. Dora seems to know what Sadie is feeling. Sadie can finish Dora's sentences.

The best part of being twins for the children is that they always have a playmate. Whether they are playing dress-up together, or are just lying on their beds reading, they are never alone. Because

Sadie and Dora are in the same developmental stage, their interests and their sense of humor are very similar. Dora and Sadie will enjoy watching *Pocahontas* or playing with Barbie dolls together. If there were an age gap between them, the older one might already have decided that Disney or dolls are not cool. Much to the dismay of their parents, Sadie and Dora will have fun getting into mischief together, too, especially tricking people about their identities.

Dora and Sadie will comfort each other and help out when they can. If Dora's speech is not clear enough, Sadie will translate her needs to the grown-ups. When Sadie is lying on her bed with a stomachache, Dora will bring her her favorite stuffed animal and run to get their parents' help. Twins often serve as a security blanket for each other. At the park, at a new day camp, or when they are flying alone on a plane to visit their grandma, they give each other a feeling of safety.

Sadie and Dora can be very protective of each other, too. Even if Sadie knows that Dora was trying to smuggle a marker from school under her shirt, she will come to Dora's defense ("Oh! She brought that from home!"). Even when Dora is angry at Sadie for wearing her new necklace, she will still cover up for her with their parents ("It wasn't Sadie who spilled the juice on the carpet. It was the baby-sitter"). In a showdown between Sadie and some kids on the block, Dora might threaten the other kids, "You touch her and I'll punch you."

Twins learn a great deal from each other. Parents are simply awestruck when one twin takes her first steps, the other watches, and within seconds begins walking, too. Dora might teach Sadie how to whistle. Sadie might teach Dora how to snap her fingers. The children will bounce ideas off each other and swap information all day long.

Twins are so much a part of each other's lives that when they are separated for any length of time, they can feel at a loss. If Sadie is riding her bike around the corner and is taking too long to return home, Dora may begin to worry. If Dora is away for the weekend at karate camp, Sadie may find herself waking up during the night to look for her or asking her, "Did you see that?" when she is lying on the couch watching TV.

Sadie and Dora can benefit tremendously from being twins. They will grow up feeling special because everyone will give them attention wherever they go. Besides the fact that they will always have someone to laugh with and talk to, they will be learning how to share, negotiate conflicts, and see the world through another person's eyes. As they grow, they can use these important skills to develop close, rewarding relationships with others.

But Dora and Sadie face certain challenges, too. Since there is always another sibling around, a twin can feel a lack of attention from her parents, a need to compete, or to feel valuable, and an urgency to define her own identity.

If the parents work hard to make sure that each child feels loved and that each child is given the opportunity to develop her own individuality, the children will enjoy growing up as twins.

Two Minutes Apart

Eleven-year-old Katherine is two minutes older than her identical twin, Lily. They are shopping at the store for Mom. Katherine holds on to the shopping list and the money because she is the oldest. Lily pushes the cart.

A truly amazing phenomenon occurs with twins. In my clinical observations, I have found that even when there are only two minutes between their births, the children's birth order takes on tremendous psychological importance. The firstborn twin and the secondborn twin may even assume the roles they would have if there were years between them.

The firstborn twin feels very special because she is number one and is often the more dominant and self-assured child (although sometimes the larger twin can take on this role, too). The secondborn twin, sometimes treated as the baby, can literally feel second-best and inferior to her sibling, and feel dominated and rejected by her, too.

In some cases, you might observe the twins interacting just like any older and younger sibling. The older twin may be bragging about her exploits, putting down everything the younger one says or does, and bossing her sibling around. The younger one will be trying desperately to equal the older one and win her approval.

Why does this happen?

In part, this has to do with the children's own identity issues. Because Katherine and Lily are twins and so many things feel the same, their age gap may be one of the only major differences between them that they can point to. Since first tends to be equated with best and twins are so competitive, Katherine has something to hold over Lily, too. "You're my little sister," she might tease her. Defensively, Lily may retort, "Mommy said I was supposed to come out first." It is interesting to note that this birth order positioning arises even when there is an older child already in the family. That's because twins function as such a separate entity unto themselves. Sometimes, though, twins will refer to each other as the second and third child, too, especially when they need ammunition.

Parents can also foster this birth order setup, by frequently referring to the twins as the oldest and youngest, always honoring the oldest one first (for instance, singing "Happy Birthday" to Katherine before Lily), or giving Katherine special responsibilities or privileges. With these actions, the parents may inadvertently have a tremendous impact upon their children's emotional experience.

For example, if they always give Katherine the shopping list and money because "she is the oldest," they convey that she has a special status and is in fact more capable of handling things. Then, because Katherine feels important and gets more experience in taking charge, she can actually become more responsible and self-confident. Since Lily is never given the chance, she will not learn these skills and may even feel incapable of taking on responsibility. If, on top of everything, the parents make constant comparisons (for example, Katherine is the reliable one but Lily is so disorganized), they will enhance these self-perceptions and profoundly affect the children's self-esteem and success in life. Perhaps parents of twins engage in these behaviors because they are caught up in following the commonly held "natural order of things," or because they are unconsciously projecting all their expectations and hopes onto their firstborn child, just as many other parents do.

There are other sources for this birth order positioning, too. Once parents have twins, they may decide that two children in the family are enough. Desiring both an older and younger child, they might assign these roles to their children. Sometimes, too, life circumstances will be a contributing factor. If there is a divorce or the death of a parent in the family, the older twin may feel it is her place to take charge; she may even assume a parental role.

Effect on the Child's Development

Like other younger siblings, Lily can go through life feeling inadequate. In her struggle to feel more valuable, she may become highly competitive with Katherine and others as she grows. However, the moment she finds the competition too tough, she may drop out of the race. If she must always follow Katherine's lead, she may grow up dependent upon others, have a hard time taking charge, and easily become enraged when she feels she is being bossed around.

As with other firstborns, Katherine's self-confidence and her leadership abilities can bring her much success. As a matter of fact, in my professional experience, I have found that in many families the firstborn twin is more academically successful. At the same time, like Lily, Katherine may struggle with competitive feelings her whole life. She will be very jealous of Lily if Lily is continuously babied in the family and feel threatened by Lily's achievements because she fears that her sister might surpass her. Like any older sibling, Katherine can develop a domineering, critical side to her personality and use it to maintain the upper hand with her sister and with others. These characteristics may cause recurring problems in her relationships as she grows.

What Parents Can Do

Deemphasize their age difference. The question arises: What would happen if twins did not know who was born first and thought that they were both lifted out at the same time?

Since this is probably not a viable way to explain things, perhaps the best thing that you can do for your twins is to deemphasize their age difference. Terms such as the "oldest twin" and the "youngest twin" should rarely be used. When you introduce the children or inscribe their names on their birthday cake, make sure to alternate the order of their names.

Foster your children's positive self-esteem. Giving each one the chance to put money in the parking meter or to take charge when the parent steps out can help each twin grow up feeling confident. Be careful not to praise either twin at the other's expense. Otherwise, one child will feel less valuable than her sibling.

Monitor the children's interactions. Intervene with your older twin if he is acting domineering, critical, or rejecting toward his sibling. Bolster your younger twin when he shows signs of feeling less competent. (See Chapters Two and Three for specific suggestions.) If your firstborn twin seems anxious about your secondborn twin's accomplishments, explain to him that his brother's achievements will not diminish your love for him.

Give your children plenty of reassurance. You will need to acknowledge how important your children's age difference seems to them while helping them see that it has to do with a wish to feel different or special. At the same time, you must reassure the children that the two-minute difference means nothing to you—you love them equally.

"I Can Do Anything Better Than You"

🪲 *Dad is walking nine-year-olds Claudine and Daniel to school. Claudine starts telling Dad a story about how she taught their dog Sparky to roll over that afternoon. Within seconds, Daniel interrupts and describes how he got Sparky to run after his bone the day before. Very quickly, the children's voices get louder as they compete for Dad's attention and Dad gets a major headache.*

Since the beginning, there have been two babies needing a diaper change, and two babies crying to be fed. For their exhausted, often distraught parents, getting through the day with both babies well taken care of became the goal.

Under these circumstances, finding an opportunity to sit alone with one baby for any length of time was extremely difficult. As "get-into-everything" toddlers and "I can do anything" preschoolers, the twins continued to require much attention, and stealing private moments alone with each remained a big problem.

While it is hard for all parents of two to give their children enough individual attention, it can be somewhat easier when there is an age gap. Because they are at different developmental stages, when the parents are busy with the younger one, the older one may find it easier to wait and even keep himself busy. While the younger one is asleep, Mom and Dad can spend time with the older one. Unlike twins, each child will be the center of attention on his birthday!

Daniel and Claudine fight hard for their parents' attention. When Dad walks in at the end of the day, each twin will practically do handstands to grab his attention, and when Mom sits down on the couch, each will casually try to lie across her lap.

The children find creative ways to get more from their parents, too. Daniel might wait until Claudine falls asleep and then sneak downstairs to the living room for an extra cuddle or two with Mom and Dad. Claudine might volunteer to run errands with Dad or feign a tummy ache so she can stay at home with Mom. Some twins will insist upon having their own birthday cakes or birthday parties at an early age.

Like any two siblings, Claudine and Daniel feel jealous when they sense that the other one is getting something extra. But for twins, feelings of jealousy and competitiveness can be more intense than for other siblings. After all, since they were little and were two adorable twins sitting next to each other in their double stroller, they have constantly been compared. And what happened if one was cuter or smiled more? He got more admiration and the other one felt upset.

One of the most difficult issues that twins face is that since they are always at the same learning stage, sooner or later one will be more advanced than the other in something. If Daniel starts riding a two-wheeler before Claudine, he will receive a great deal of attention and Claudine may end up feeling less competent. Claudine may decide that because Daniel started first or because she cannot seem to ride as well, this is his domain and she may refuse to try. This kind of a pattern can actually deter her development and repeat itself throughout her life.

When Daniel and Claudine enter school, their rivalry will intensify, especially if they are in the same class. The two will try hard to outdo each other in every way. If Claudine gets better grades in language, Daniel might either study hard to surpass her or throw all his efforts into science, where he feels certain he can win out. Even when they are not in the same class, because they stand out as twins and often share the same friends and teachers, their progress will be common knowledge. And how will either twin feel if one makes it into the gifted class and the other does not?

Like any jealous siblings, twins will constantly try to top the other's stories, play with or wear whatever the other one picks up, or put the other down (for instance, saying, "The music you listen to is not cool"). Jealous twins have been known to kick, punch, and pull each other's hair, too.

Because the two children are so closely bonded, at times they may feel ambivalent about competing with each other. Despite the fact that Claudine wants to be number one, she may not dare to outdo Daniel in tennis because she fears that he will get angry with her; after all tennis is his territory, and she may be afraid to upset him.

Effect on the Child's Development

Daniel can transfer his competitive feelings from Claudine to friends, coworkers, or the driver in the car next to him. Claudine may struggle hard her whole life to be at the top wherever she goes, feel stressed all the time, and suffer tremendously whenever she feels defeated. Throughout life, both twins may continue to feel insecure in areas in which they felt less competent than their sibling. Some twins remain very conflicted about competition their whole lives, because as children they saw it as harmful to their sibling. As a result, they may strenuously avoid competition and even give up some of their aspirations.

What Parents Can Do

Spend time alone with each child. Though it is hard work, it is essential that you spend time alone with each of your twins. Sitting and reading to one child while the other is occupied by your spouse, a playmate, or a baby-sitter will bring you closer and reassure each child that he or she is important to you. Some parents will arrange a private "date" with each child once a month. The parent and child choose a special activity, such as going to a museum, mark it on the calendar, and have it to look forward to. You might find that planning a dinner out alone with one child from time to time will give you an opportunity to talk about issues and to see what is on your child's mind. You both will feel more connected.

Give according to the children's needs. Sometimes parents of twins believe strongly that if they spend fifteen minutes with one twin, they must spend exactly fifteen minutes with the other, and they feel very troubled when this is impossible. While most parents acknowledge that they should make sure that each child gets enough attention, they find that what works best is giving according to the child's needs and not an equality plan. If you must spend some extra time with one child because she has had a hard day, explain to the other child that sometimes you need to give one of them a little more attention than the other. Remind him, too, of situations in which he received extra help.

Acknowledge your children's feelings. Communicate to your children that feeling jealousy and anger toward their twin is natural. All siblings have these feelings. Convey to them, too, that you understand that it is hard for them to be twins because they have to share their parents' love and are always being compared.

Set limits on your children's behavior. Intervene to stop your children when they are engaging in critical, domineering, rejecting, or aggressive behaviors toward each other. Help them to understand that this behavior stems from their jealous and angry feelings. They must use positive ways to express themselves instead, such as talking about their feelings with each other or coming to you for help.

Try to place your twins in separate classes. If you can, choose a school that has more than one class to each grade. Once they are separated, each child will have an opportunity to develop her own abilities without the hindrance of constantly being compared to her twin.

Avoid comparisons. Comparisons make children feel awful. If you call one of your twins the "neat one" and the other one "the slob," or use phrases such as "Why can't you be as organized as your brother?," neither child will benefit. The twin who is not measuring up will feel less loved and angry. The one who is being lauded will feel pressure to live up to this label and guilty because he is feeling good at his sibling's expense. It is better to deal with each child separately, instead. In privacy, you might tell one, "I like the way you are keeping your room in order," or the other, "I think we need to help you find a place for each of your things so your room will be easier to manage."

Caution friends, relatives, and teachers to avoid comparing the children, too. This will diminish the competition between the children.

Do not display preferential treatment to either child. Though it is natural to switch your preference from one twin to another from time to time, it is important to monitor your approaches. If one is more outgoing and funny, and you prefer this behavior because she is more like you, be careful. You may unconsciously be showing favoritism. Try to find qualities in each of your twins that you can enjoy.

Be alert to your child's inadequacy feelings. If one child is not handing in his math homework while his brother is winning math awards, there is probably a connection. If your child complains that he is not good at math, you will not make him feel better by immediately pointing out, "Yes, but you are good in reading." This statement will confirm his worst fear about math, and about being less competent than his brother, and increase the likelihood that he will continue to have difficulties. Instead, explain to him that each child proceeds at his own pace in learning. Encourage him to try by saying, "Don't worry. If you keep working at it, you will succeed." You can point out that maybe his sibling has a particular talent in math, but he might, too. There is room for two successful algebra students in the family. Then you can point out areas in which he is already successful, to boost his self-esteem.

Reassure your children of your love. Explain to them that you do not measure their value according to who can do something better. They are each special individuals with wonderful qualities, and you will always love them both.

Who Are We?

🐞 *Four-year-old fraternal twins Josh and David are jamming with their father who is a professional drummer. Josh bangs away on his own set of drums while David sits nearby keeping time on the keyboard.*

Even when twins are not identical, family, friends, and teachers will mix them up. If everyone else has such a hard time making a clear distinction, so will the twins.

Society tends to add to twins' identity confusion by portraying them as if they were one person. Magazine articles and TV talk shows regularly feature stories in which one twin from Iowa feels pain when his twin in Arizona, from whom he was separated at birth, is stabbed. These kinds of tales prompt children to question twins, "Do you feel it when your twin gets punched?" or "Do you have the same brain?" How is a twin to feel like a separate person?

But twins can be confused about their identities even without outside influence. As babies, twins have been known to lie in a crib sucking each other's thumbs. Identical toddlers have been seen stopping abruptly in their tracks, in utter confusion, when running past each other. Sharing the same room, the same clothes, and the same birthday can make the two children feel as if they are one person. Sometimes, they may lose sight of where one of them begins and the other leaves off.

The fact that Josh and David are often treated as a unit does not help. When calling the roll, teachers will ask, "Are the twins in school today?" Since it is easier for their parents, David and Josh may always be taken to the same swim classes and playdates. As a result, the twins may develop a clearly defined "twindividuality," and have a harder time establishing their own separate identities.

Even though they are twins, each child is different. One child will be more active; one will be more social. One twin will have exceptional musical abilities; the other will be gifted in writing. Some of this has to do with the children's innate temperament and abilities. But as they grow, there will be other factors shaping them.

As with any two siblings, Josh and David's identities will form in relation to each other. David may try to be just like Josh and copy everything he does, or he may choose to find his own niche by doing something completely different. They might both end up taking classes in art, but Josh will paint and David will sculpt. If David is very mischievous and frequently gets into trouble with their parents, Josh may try to be the perfect angel. It is interesting to note that studies of identical twins have shown them to be more alike when they are separated at birth than when they live together. When they are apart, they are not trying to polarize to be different.

Parents' labels also help create the twins' identities. If Josh can talk first, he may be labeled the smart one. If David is more active and is always getting into things, he may be called the naughty twin. Even the way a child is described when he was in utero or during birth ("He just pushed his brother to the side") affects the way the child sees himself and develops. In their relentless comparisons of the two children, teachers, friends, and family members will either reinforce these labels or come up with their own.

If these labels stick, as they usually do, they can become the children's self-definitions and turn into self-fulfilling prophecies.

Parents can also project onto their twins different identities having to do with their own early childhood experiences. A parent might label his oldest twin, Josh, the aggressive baby, because he always grabs the younger one's toys. Unconsciously, Josh may remind the parent of his older brother who always pushed him around.

Effect on the Child's Development

Throughout life David and Josh will search for ways to feel unique. David may wear two different colored socks each day. Josh may keep his hair long or act wild. During the adolescent years, when all children are struggling to define themselves, Josh and David may actively push each other away by criticizing each other mercilessly, arguing nonstop, or avoiding each other completely.

Besides giving them some breathing space, this distancing behavior serves other purposes for twins. Like all teenagers, David and Josh will feel very awkward and insecure about themselves and will constantly be scrutinizing their personalities. Since Josh and David are so alike, they may identify traits, gestures, or mannerisms in each other that they do not like in themselves and unconsciously decide that if they disengage from their twin, they will rid themselves of these characteristics. Boy and girl twins will have an added impetus to detach from each other. At this stage, their budding sexuality will create sexual urges between them.

Interestingly enough, at the same time that the twins are desperately fighting to feel separate, they may experience some ambivalence about letting go. It is common for a twin to feel angry and criticize her sibling's friends and other outside interests because she feels abandoned or feels guilty because she wants some independence.

As young adults, one twin may move far away from the other or even get a nose job. Later on in life, however, after each twin establishes a more solid sense of self, the two may come together again and become good friends.

Sometimes twins never really separate psychologically, though. Because they feel so comfortable together or because life's circumstances have made them rely too heavily upon each other, they may each consider their twins their major relationship. Although this relationship can be positive for both individuals, it may have a disastrous effect on each twin's development. If the twins continue to play out negative childhood roles with each other (for instance, one is very dominant while the other always remains passive), neither will grow emotionally.

Even if one twin happens to get married, his twin may still maintain too great an importance in his life. Some adults will admit that in an emergency they will call their twin before their spouse. If the unmarried twin cannot tolerate sharing his sibling, he may unconsciously test his sibling's loyalty in an attempt to undermine the marriage.

What Parents Can Do

Help others to know who is who. Early on, try to make it easier for others to identify your children. If you always dress them exactly alike, or comb their hair the same way, it will lead to confusion. When they are small, some parents embroider the first letter of their children's names on their clothing, or dress each one in a different range of colors to facilitate their recognition.

Treat your children as individuals. It will help the children to feel more separate if you avoid using the term "the twins" all the time. It is better to use their names. Instruct others to do the same.

Help each child develop her own interests, too. Even though it is easier to bring both twins to one place, if a child wants to register for a different program, or study a different instrument, try to give her this opportunity. Putting the children in separate classes at school will give them a tremendous opportunity to blossom as individuals.

Help each twin to have his or her own privacy. Twins might prefer to have separate rooms, or to partition their shared room as they get older (especially opposite-sex twins), and it is important to make these options available. Allow each child to have a confidential relationship with you, too, unless there is a serious issue that must be communicated to the other child.

Give each child his or her own possessions. During different phases of their development, twins may have the same interests and desire the same things. But sharing all the time is very hard for children. Some parents find that having two of many items works best. This helps the children to feel more separate, and reduces the frequency of battles. Large items, such as a TV or a computer, can be shared.

Do not force the twins to be different. If they want to dress alike from time to time, to join the same hockey team, or to sleep in one room, that is fine—as long as they are aware that they can make other choices.

Avoid labeling your children. It is better to describe your child's behavior rather than label his personality. For example, you might tell your relatives, "David cries when he feels hurt," rather than saying, "He's the sensitive twin." Otherwise, the behaviors and the children's identities will become etched in stone. Try to view your children's behaviors as only temporary, too. Today, one of your twins bites when he is upset. Tomorrow he will have better control. If you label him aggressive or naughty, he may not change. It is crucial, too, to analyze how your own personal history colors your view of each of your twins, so you can relate to them more objectively.

Birthdays. To give each child the feeling that she is special, you can have two separate cakes, sing "Happy Birthday" twice, or make some sort of special celebration for each child. Try to encourage friends and relatives to send them separate cards and presents. Involving the children in choosing their gifts is important, too.

Sometimes the children will be happiest with exactly the same presents, while at other times they may want similar, or completely different ones.

Involve the children in decision making. Let each twin take part in choosing his own clothing, the color of his room, or where he would like to go with you on a special outing. This will help each child to develop his own preferences.

Schedule some individual activities. Sending each twin on separate sleepovers at their grandparents' house will help them feel like independent individuals.

Discuss identity issues with your children. Talk with your children about how hard it can be for twins to establish their own identities. Alert them to the fact that sometimes they might get angry and push each other away because they are trying to feel separate. Help the child who is doing the pushing not to feel guilty about her wish to feel separate while encouraging her to be sensitive to her sibling's feelings. Provide support to the child who is being rejected and reassure her that there is nothing wrong with her.

Help each child find himself. No matter what you do, siblings will form their identities in relation to each other. But if you give each child ample opportunities for self-discovery and a good feeling about his own abilities, while helping him keep his doors wide open (even if his twin is great in baseball, it does not mean that he cannot play), he will be more inner-directed.

Just the Two of Us

Three-year-old identical twins Ian and Ross are constructing with Legos in one corner of their nursery classroom. They whisper suggestions to each other and laugh at their own private jokes. From time to time, other children meander over, but the twins rarely include them in their play.

Ian and Ross keep each other company when Mom and Dad are sleeping, at work, or busy doing chores. Since it can be an ordeal to take both of them to the supermarket, they often stay at home with the sitter. Parents feel less of a need to set up playdates for their twins, because they are already getting plenty of social experience. As a result, Ross and Ian can develop a rather insular life together.

Since they feel most comfortable with each other, Ross and Ian might stick together when they go to the park or when they start day camp, and not seek out any other relationships. Even if there is an older sibling in the home, the twins will mostly keep to themselves. (The older child may have withdrawn from his siblings anyway, because she feels so overwhelmed and outnumbered by them.) Consequently, the children may end up not knowing how to form new friendships or join in on other children's play.

As they grow, socializing may be hard for the twins for other reasons. Because they are already two, the moment a playmate visits, a triangular situation arises. Ross and Ian may end up competing to be the other child's best friend. And what happens if one of the twins gets along better with their guest? The other twin can feel devastated.

Other potent scenarios will arise, too. If Ian forms a special friendship with another child when they are on a summer vacation, Ross may feel left out. He might feel very jealous about sharing Ian and angry at Ian because he prefers to be with someone else. If Ross is invited to fewer birthday parties, because he is either less outgoing or too bossy, he can end up feeling inferior to Ian. To make matters worse, if Ian is the more dominant twin, he may try to take over any friend of Ross's who walks in the door.

It will be mortifying for Ian if Ross teams up with other kids in the schoolyard when they are picking on him. This might happen if Ross is trying to win friends or separate psychologically from Ian. Such issues can become more intense during their adolescent years, when one or both of them urgently wants his own separate life.

Though two children with an age gap will encounter similar complications, especially when they are very close in age, these difficulties are more prevalent for twins because their relationship is more intense and they tend to travel in the same social circles.

Effect on the Child's Development

Many twins grow up and maintain a close, pleasurable bond with each other; yet, they are very social and develop other satisfying relationships, too. Others may feel socially awkward and have a hard time forming relationships. In some cases, twins may continue to see each other as their primary relationship throughout life. As adults, they might look to each other to go to the movies, go shopping, and to vacation with, and they may never marry or commit themselves to a long-term relationship with another person.

What Parents Can Do

Provide ample opportunities for socialization. Enroll your children in play groups and nursery school early on and be sure to arrange plenty of playdates for them. As difficult as it can be, try to help each twin develop her own separate social life, too. You can encourage each one to go on separate playdates or attend after-school programs alone.

When your children are at day camp, it is best to have the children placed in separate groups, so that each child can learn how to start up a relationship, join in on group play, determine her own taste in friends, and form her own social identity. If she is too busy looking over her shoulder to see if her sibling is surrounded by more kids, she will not get the same opportunity.

Monitor your children's playdates. When one child has a playdate and wants privacy, try to keep the other one entertained or invite a friend for him to play with, too. When the children have a guest and they are all playing together, observe their interactions closely. You should intervene if the children are not able to work through conflicts or if one of your twins is being excluded. Provide emotional support to one who feels left out and coach him on what he can do or say to handle the situation. Reassure your twins that when they form other friendships, they do not take away from their love for each other.

Growing up as twins can be truly wonderful for children. The children always have a best friend, and at an early age they learn important social skills that will help them in life. Finding a way for each to develop his or her own unique individuality is the hard part. With their parents' help, though, the children can grow up feeling very close to each other, while creating rich, fulfilling, separate lives.

6

The Only Child

Five-year-old Christopher is walking down the street hand in hand with his mom and dad. "One, two, three," everyone counts when they arrive at a curb—and his parents swing him on top. "Did you see how high I jumped?" he asks excitedly. "Oh! Christopher. That was wonderful!" his parents respond in unison.

Growing up on his own, Christopher has the major benefit of having his parents' undivided attention. He never has to compete with any sisters or brothers for his parents' love—he is number one for life. Christopher's parents cherish him and consider him to be the moon and the stars. Mom and Dad are more available to listen to him, and he will get whatever there is to give.

Because there is no other child making demands, Mom and Dad can pay closer attention to any difficulties that he is having. They are more patient, too, when Christopher is refusing to get dressed or flings his toys around in anger, and help him work through his emotions.

Not only can the parents be more attentive to Christopher's emotional needs, but because they have only one child, they have more time, energy, and economic resources available for him.

Christopher will be more likely to go to better schools and the college of his choice (perhaps free of student loans), and his parents will be able to offer him more assistance when he starts his own family. And when it comes time for an inheritance, everything goes to him. He will not have to endure any bitter sibling battles.

As a result of all this positive attention, Christopher can grow up feeling close to his parents and good about himself. He will believe that he can do just about anything, and probably become a high achiever in life. After all, children internalize the way their parents feel about them, and this becomes the way they feel about themselves.

If his parents handle him carefully and provide him with ample love and support, he will grow up benefiting from his special position in life.

"You're All We've Got"

🐾 *Christopher is practicing writing "Chris" on a piece of paper, just for fun. "That R is backwards," says Dad, glancing over his shoulder. "Don't you remember the way I showed you? Write it again." Christopher refuses to do so, Dad gets angry, and the two battle back and forth. Finally, Christopher rips up his paper.*

Along with the benefits of being an only child, there are some challenges that Christopher may face. Growing up without siblings, Christopher might feel lonely and may lack experience in relating to peers. His adoring parents might overpraise him, fail to set limits with him, or jump in too quickly to solve his problems. As a result, Christopher may end up having unrealistic expectations of himself and others, feeling dependent, and lacking in important social skills. To remedy these problems, it is essential that his parents create ample social opportunities for him, give him a realistic view of himself, teach him basic social skills, set limits with him, and encourage his independence.

Being the sole focus of his parents' attention can also raise another potential problem. As we saw in Chapter Two, parents may consciously or unconsciously place too much pressure on their firstborn child to achieve. With an only child, however, this pressure can be raised several notches. After all, they may see this as their only chance to raise a great kid (especially if they have waited a long time to have children or have had a hard time conceiving or adopting him). Any unresolved needs that the parents may have to feel worthwhile and successful in the world are riding on Christopher, too, so he must be perfect in every way.

The spoken or unspoken message to Christopher may be, "You're all we have. You have to succeed in everything," and Christopher, who wants to please his parents and be loved more than anything, may fear letting his parents down.

With only one child to focus on, the parents may scrutinize Christopher's behavior too much. Inappropriate demands made upon a small child to act like a little adult can cause him to feel that he is inadequate and lead to exhaustive, upsetting battles between parent and child. Christopher might resist his parents' demands tooth and nail in an effort to reestablish his self-respect. If there were more children in the family, the parents would spread their demands out a little more. However, because the firstborn child keeps entering new territories all the time, there is a tendency for his anxious parents to continue to evaluate his performance more stringently.

Interestingly enough, some parents end up giving their child a double message. They may praise him to the sky and tell him he is capable of doing anything, but because they critique his every breath on a daily basis, they also give him the feeling that he is a failure. This concurrent idealization and devaluation can ultimately undermine the child's confidence in himself (in either case, he has no clue as to his true self-worth), and undo his chances for success.

Effect on the Child's Development

It is clear that such intense parental pressure gives the child the message that only if he achieves will he be loved; causes him to develop a harsh, unaccepting approach toward himself and others; and makes it hard for him to relax and enjoy life. As a result, some only children ultimately leave home at an early age to "get out from underneath their parents' thumb." Many will become highly driven and successful in their careers, despite the fact that they still feel insecure inside, while others drop out entirely because they are afraid to fail, or feel resentful toward their parents. Some only children feel conflicted about success their whole lives.

What Parents Can Do

There are many ways that you can reduce the pressure that you are placing on your only child or avoid it completely.

Show him that you love him unconditionally. When he does not get a perfect test score or he strikes out at bat, respond in a calm, accepting way. Tell him, "Don't worry, it happens" or "You'll do better next time." He will know that no matter what, you will still love him. This will help him build up his frustration tolerance. He will learn not to be so hard on himself, or give up too easily. If you always point out the negatives and correct him instead, he will conclude that no matter how hard he tries, he will not be good enough for you.

Give her support. You might tell her that you can see that it is often hard for her to be the only child, because she is constantly comparing herself to you. But she will be able to do the same things that you can do when she grows up. Talking openly and noncritically about your own mistakes will also help her to be more accepting of herself.

Identify why you are pressuring him so hard. If you are pressuring him too hard in any area—for example, driving him crazy about forgetting his school books at school—try to get in touch with your reasons why. There is usually a personal issue involved with a very strong parental reaction. Perhaps one of you was called "irresponsible" by a parent or teacher when you were small and you do not want him to experience the pain you did or "be the same way." If so, take a deep breath and a huge step back, so that you can face the situation more objectively. You and he are separate individuals, and you each will have different experiences in life. Help him develop the skills he needs to cope.

Avoid comparisons. Try not to compare your child to your friends' children, her cousins, or the neighbor's kids across the street. Whether she is told, or overhears, that she is better than everyone else or worse, in the long run she will suffer.

Learn about your child's stage of development. The more you understand his natural capabilities, the more appropriate your demands of your child will be. Knowing that children do forget to brush their teeth and do rush through their homework will help you take a calmer approach. Expect resistance, too—for example, when you tell him to turn off the TV or clean up his room. Children need to assert themselves so that they can feel independent. They are not robots! Rather than explode, give him advance warning, choices, and time to comply.

Two Against One

🐛 *Mom and Dad are arguing over whether or not Christopher is old enough to go on a sleepover at his friend's house. Tempers flare, their voices rise, and Christopher retreats deeper and deeper into himself. Then, out of sheer desperation, he suddenly declares, "I don't want to go!"*

There are many natural emotional complexities to the relationship between a parent and a child. But when a child grows up alone in a family with one or two parents, the relationships can be more intense and cause the child much stress.

In any family, children often bear the brunt of their parents' emotional issues. But an only child goes it alone. If either parent is a fearful person, his or her anxieties may be passed on to the child, too.

Parents love their children and naturally make them the center of their lives. But this can lead to some problems for Christopher, who is the sole source of parental gratification. Though it's natural for parents to feel concern about their children's welfare, with only one child parents can easily go too far. If Christopher's parents become hysterical over every pain, problem, or challenge that he experiences, they may fail to provide him with the emotional support he needs, and even make him more anxious. Christopher may end up feeling that he must be the one to watch out for their feelings, instead. He may even decide that it's better to withhold information from them, and stop turning to them for help altogether.

Because there will be no other children coming along after him, his parents may have a harder time letting go of Christopher and hold on to him too tight for too long. However well-meaning, they may become intrusive and try to control his every choice, even whom he will date. He may end up feeling responsible for their emotional well-being and guilty about any independent move he makes.

Triangular relationships are difficult in any situation. But the setup between two adults and one child can be particularly intense. Christopher may feel very overwhelmed if his parents constantly line up against him or are always arguing over what to do with him. Sometimes, too, a parent will seek an alliance with the child against an out-of-favor spouse, use the child as a sounding board, or try to enlist him as the marital mediator. Such roles cause severe loyalty conflicts for the child.

Effect on the Child's Development

Many only children struggle to establish boundaries with their parents throughout their adult lives. A fear of engulfment and a desperate need for independence, carried over from their home lives, may make it hard for them to form intimate adult relationships, too. As soon as someone starts getting close to them or begins to make demands on them, they might flee.

Some of these parent-child issues can be played out with any firstborn child, but once a second sibling is born, she balances out the equation. It becomes an "us and them" situation, which dilutes the intensity of family relationships. Besides, there are two children to meet their parents' needs.

What Parents Can Do

Take responsibility for your behavior. If you have had a hard day at work and you end up screaming at your child, be sure to apologize to him, explain the reason why, and let him know that he did nothing wrong. Be careful not to transfer your own fears to your child. If you are afraid of heights, do not talk about your anxiety in front of your child.

Avoid overreacting to every difficulty your child faces. Your child needs your help. If her best friend tells her she will never play with her again, stay calm. Tell her, "That must have been hard for you," or "You must have felt hurt." Reassure her that sometimes children get angry at each other and then make up the next day. Suggest some viable strategies that she might use, such as playing with another friend if it happens again. You will be teaching her how to cope.

Do not gang up on your child. He will feel outnumbered and overwhelmed. Try having only one parent at a time instructing him about a rule. If you and your spouse are in disagreement over how to handle your child, try not to argue in front of him. Have private discussions whenever possible.

Treat your child as a child. Do not turn to her to fulfill your adult needs for love and support.

Establish clear boundaries. Make a distinction between your marital relationship and your relationship with your child. This will dilute the emotional intensity of the parent-child relationship. If yours is a single-parent family, it is important to include other adults in your home life and to build your own social life, too.

Whenever a marital or a family problem arises, communicate to your child that it is not his problem. The adults will handle it.

Let her go. It is crucial to give your child the following messages: "Go out into the world. It is safe and you can manage." Allow your child to choose her own paths in life, too. If you are too controlling, she may end up confused about what she truly wants to do.

You can comfort yourself by keeping in mind that as children grow and separate, we do not lose them. No matter how big your child gets, he will need you forever.

One of the major challenges with only children is not to push them ahead too hard or hold them back. If parents give them positive attention, encouragement, and plenty of opportunities to grow, they will benefit from being only children and build happy, successful lives.

7

Family Size Makes a Difference

Everyone loves to read about the loving interactions among the sisters in *Little Women*. The image of a huge, close-knit family seated around the dinner table, chatting happily about their days, stirs the fantasies of all, especially those who come from a small family. There is no question that a large family offers children much. There are more people to love and to turn to for support. When things work well, each child gains a positive sense of identity and feels security in the family.

But growing up in the happiest of large families carries with it many difficult challenges for children and parents. More children means more physical and emotional needs, and everyone must share the family's resources—money, possessions, living space, and the parents' love and attention. And with each additional child, the parents become more and more overloaded and stressed, and it can be harder for them to meet each child's emotional needs.

In this chapter we will see how having more children in the family enhances the birth order challenges that children are already facing and how you can help your children feel more comfortable.

The Oldest of Many

In Chapter Two, we observed Rachel as she tried to adapt to having a younger brother and to her role as an older sibling. But what happened to her after Jenny, the third child of the family, was born, and what would life be like for any oldest child if her mom and dad kept on having babies?

The oldest would probably continue to enjoy many of the positives of her role. She would still be the one to gain the privileges of staying up late, opening a bank account, and riding the subway before everyone else. She might even be the first to have a room of her own. Her parents would probably get very involved with her when she applies to college and make a big deal when she goes out on her first date, too.

However, with each successive birth of a new sibling, the child must share the parents' attention even more. As he watches his parents become increasingly overloaded, the oldest child can see the old treasured central focus of attention that he once knew slipping further and further away, and he might feel resentful.

Some oldest siblings will declare, "I wanted to be the only child, but my parents wouldn't listen to me," or "My second brother was the straw that broke the camel's back. I felt there was no room for me." Others claim amnesia about their siblings' births.

Interestingly enough, some oldest siblings (especially girls), seem to have more positive feelings about the birth of their second sibling than their first. Often the second birth occurs when the oldest child is between the age of six and eight and the child views the younger sibling as her baby doll. Whereas she was too young to take care of her first sibling, she may dress the youngest one or brush her hair, so she will naturally bond with her more. Since the oldest is more immediately threatened by the child closest in age to her, she may also feel relieved that her parents' focus has moved off the second child. It is clear that the child's negative and positive reactions to having more brothers and sisters can coexist.

An oldest child can find her parents' preoccupation with her younger siblings very difficult. If she has found waiting for her parents to be too frustrating, or she does not want to stress them any further (especially when she knows that they will get angry with her if she becomes demanding), the oldest may decide to deal with her successes, problems, and emotional pain all alone. Courtney, the twelve-year-old oldest sister of five, states, "I just got used to not having attention." Not only can the oldest feel angry about not getting enough attention, she may feel jealous because everyone seems so taken with her teeny baby sister, her chatterbox toddler brother, and her four-year-old sister dressed in Mary Janes.

In an effort to win attention in the family, the oldest may try to be a very good boy, drive himself hard to be great at everything he does, or become superhelpful to his parents. He may have learned early on that the way to gain approval is to do what his parents want and to be very grown-up.

With several children looking up to her, the oldest child of many may experience even more pressure from her parents to "set a good example." Because she is the trailblazer for the rest, her parents may believe that if she does well at school or behaves correctly, everyone else will follow suit.

Overloaded parents with large families often turn to their oldest child for help. In some families, the oldest is just required to do some simple chores, such as vacuuming the living room rug, while in others, a seven-year-old who has four younger siblings may be required to help feed, diaper, and baby-sit the babies. In some cases, the oldest child must drop out of school to support the family and give up any dreams about going to college.

At the same time that the oldest child is trying to fulfill his difficult role in the family, he faces constant inequities that cause him much resentment. Every time all the children are running around wild, he may be the only one reprimanded. "You are old enough to know better." While he washes the dinner dishes, his younger siblings may run off and switch on the TV. Frequently, he cannot walk to the park with a friend without taking along one or two of his younger siblings. When he buys a bag of potato chips for himself and the others start whining, he is told, "Just give them some."

The oldest child may have to make big sacrifices, too. She might have to give up her friends, because her family has to move to another neighborhood where they can afford a larger house to accommodate all the children, or attend a less expensive college than the school of her choice because "the others will have to go, too."

Parents tend to be more overprotective with their oldest child, who serves as the groundbreaker for the others. Brittany, the eighteen-year-old oldest sister of four, laments, "I had to fight hard with my parents to gain any privileges. I wanted to walk to school on my own like my friends, but they did not agree until I was in seventh grade. But as soon as I did it and proved it was okay, two of my younger sisters were allowed to do it right away."

The oldest child will certainly find it harder to have privacy the more siblings he has. When he is trying to do his homework, one of his siblings may pull the pencil out of his hands while another one races off with his notebook. But he must always repress his anger because he is expected not to harm his sisters and brothers.

As a result of her experience, the oldest child of many may grow up to be a responsible, take-charge person. Unfortunately, she may also become a perfectionist because she is struggling hard to avoid making any mistakes and win her parents' favor. Consequently, as she grows, she might make undue demands upon herself and others. Because she has had to handle so much responsibility in the family, she may take on too much wherever she goes, too. She could grow up feeling that she exists to take care of everybody else, and find unthinkable the idea of buying herself a special pair of earrings or having an evening out with friends. If she feels burned out and overburdened from taking care of her siblings, she may also transfer some of this resentment to her own children.

Some oldest siblings become the hub of family life as their parents age, advising their brothers and sisters and organizing family dinners. Others flee to the opposite coast.

Helping Your Oldest Child to Feel Comfortable and Loved
You will need to communicate to your oldest child through words of praise and affection that he is loved unconditionally: she does not have to be a perfect child. It is important to address his feelings about his younger siblings' births ("First you were alone with Mom and Dad, then brother came, and now sister. Do you miss the old days?"). Help your oldest to have his own space (if possible, divide up a shared space or give him his own room) and try not to overburden him. Whenever possible, you might rely more upon your spouse and your other children, or enlist the help of a family member or a baby-sister. When you need your oldest child's help, be sure to make your requests respectfully, try to give him choices, show appreciation for his efforts, and give him as much freedom as possible. Refer back to Chapter Two for more suggestions on how to achieve these important goals.

Many in the Middle

And what happens to Michael when there are more babies after Jenny and other siblings join him in the middle? In many respects, he will continue to benefit from the pluses of being a middle child, as he did before. "I like the fact that I am not the first to try things," says Sean, the twelve-year-old second child of four. Everyone learns from the oldest sibling about what it's like to wear braces or attend the first school social long before they are actually facing the experience. As a result, the younger children are better prepared for situations and are often chomping at the bit for their opportunity. Middle children are generally less pressured or burdened with responsibility than their eldest sibling, too.

A middle child of many can turn to one of his older siblings when she needs the support of someone close in age. A forty-year-old third child of four relates, "I had someone else to talk to about sex when I was afraid to go to my parents." At the same time, the middle child still has the rich growth-producing experience of nurturing one or more younger siblings who might turn to her.

But with two, three, or even six children in the middle, many of the hardships of being a middle child will be accentuated. Having more defined positions in the family, the oldest child and the youngest will probably still command a larger portion of the family attention. So there are more opportunities for a middle child to feel overlooked and jealous. The birth of each additional sibling will be hard for middle children, too, as one by one, each child loses his position as the baby and more children must share the same room and their parents' attention.

In most families, siblings have the strongest rivalry with the children immediately adjacent to them in age. And, often, the fiercest competition in the family is between the first and the secondborn child. As Wendy, the thirteen-year-old secondborn child of four, relates, "I try hard to live up to my oldest sister's grades and be as good as her or even better." Her older sister acknowledges her end of the competition, too: "We were in ballet class together and she was skinnier and more flexible. So I dropped out." Since children pair off in older-younger relationships up and down the birth order, there are usually many rivalries going on in the family at the same time. For example, the second youngest child can feel especially jealous of the baby for robbing him of his special spot.

Like their oldest sibling, older middle children will feel resentful if they are called upon to share more caretaking responsibilities or meet higher standards than the younger ones. And if for some reason the oldest child rebels or withdraws from her role, the secondborn may end up taking over her position with all its expectations. If the oldest and the second child run off to the schoolyard, the responsibilities will be passed down the birth order. Younger middle children will be angered if the older ones have more privileges, exclude them, or push them around.

The middle children in a large family work hard to distinguish themselves. If the firstborn and secondborn children are vying for top billing as the best dancer in the family, the thirdborn might decide that she cannot compete and may take up basketball instead, while the fourth may become the outspoken child. As the laterborn middle children arrive, they will have a more difficult time finding a niche for themselves because many choice roles will have already been taken. (Sometimes being the only child of one sex can help tremendously. I discuss the effect of gender upon birth order in Chapter Nine.) Since it is natural for parents, they often label their children: the athlete, the reliable one, or the clown. While these references will certainly distinguish the children, they can also pigeonhole them and prevent them from growing, so they should be avoided.

Though it can work out that each middle child finds a positive, satisfying position in the family, the more children there are, the more likely some middle children will end up getting sidestepped. Feeling left out and unattended to, they might withdraw into themselves, fight their parents continually, or try to fulfill their needs outside the family.

Helping Your Middle Children Feel Valued

You must work extra hard with your middle children to make sure that no one feels overlooked. Checking in with each one every day—for example, "How was your day?"—is very important. So is being attuned to their feelings, helping them negotiate their rivalries, fostering their interests, being affectionate with them, and spending some time alone with each. Some parents find that involving a loving grandparent, aunt, uncle, or friend who can give extra individualized attention to the children can help each child to feel more special.

Refer back to Chapter Four for many more ideas on how to work effectively with your middle children.

The Baby

Who is it who chases after her two older brothers and flings herself on top of them as they wrestle each other to the ground? It's little Jenny—the family mascot, pet, princess.

At the other end of the spectrum from her oldest sibling, the youngest has a special spot in the family, too. As the youngest of several siblings, she always has someone to show her how to do a somersault on the living room rug, or to lift her up to the water fountain for a drink. She loves to tag along with her siblings and their friends wherever they go, and more than anything in the world, she wants to be one of the group.

The youngest child with several siblings is exposed to much more than other children her age. She watches as the older ones go off to day camp, grabs a knapsack, and says, "I go to my camp, too!" And even though she has no clue about what to do, she wants to sit down with them and play Nintendo games. By two she is already socialized and her verbal skills can be quite mature. Sometimes, when the family is sitting around the dinner table, she will convulse her siblings by reciting a long string of epithets that they have carefully taught her.

Wanting to be like the others, the littlest insists upon putting his own tape in the VCR, and may even toilet-train himself on his own at an early age. Because he is so small and always comes up against bigger kids, he develops a certain toughness and an assertiveness, too. He will shout, "Don't tease me!" or "It's my turn!" when someone gets in his way.

Since parents are so much more relaxed about childrearing by the time they have their youngest child, she may be raised in a completely opposite fashion to their oldest child. One mother relates, "We used to rush home from the mall for our firstborn's nap so that she could sleep in her crib. Our youngest sleeps in her car seat, her high chair, or on the floor, depending on what is going on. We painstakingly taught our oldest the alphabet using flash cards, but our youngest has simply learned through osmosis."

The youngest may watch endless hours of TV (even soap operas) with his older siblings, have more cookies and soda than ever was permitted, and sleep with his parents when he has a nightmare (whereas the older children were walked back to their rooms). One mother of three acknowledges, "I knew the others survived. So if I bent the rules a bit, I knew I wouldn't make her into a psycho." Sometimes, too, this more relaxed approach may have to do with the parents' recognition that this will be their last baby.

Tucked away in her baby spot, the youngest will be fairly removed from the worries and caretaking aspects of the family. It will be a long time before she is tall enough to stack the dishes in the dishwasher, or is able to unload the washing machine. Besides, there are so many hands to take care of things already. She may sense there is a family crisis going on when Dad loses his job, but as the youngest, her life will be the least affected.

Many of the positives of his position can carry some potential for negative side effects, though. Because he is the cute little pet and everyone is laxer with him about the rules, he may grow up having a hard time respecting and following rules wherever he goes. Since his parents are so busy and much more laid-back with him, they may not give him enough stimulation to move ahead. For example, they may not read to him often enough or encourage him to attend programs that will help him develop his interests. To quote a sixty-eight-year-old father of three, "With the first two, we were too intense. The third sort of grew up in benign neglect, which was both good and bad." As a result, some youngest children may not become too ambitious. However, others will in fact become very competitive and end up topping them all.

The youngest of many is often babied too much, too. Rather than encouraging her to be independent, her parents and siblings often jump in too quickly to take over for her, and she may never learn how to handle her own problems. As she grows, she may lean on her siblings to do her tough algebra assignments for her, or to bankroll her expenses when she runs up her credit card bills. If she is never given any responsibilities in the house, she will not learn how to be responsible, either. As a grown-up, in some ways she may be superindependent and in others still very much a baby.

Surrounded by older siblings who seem so much smarter and

more capable than he, the youngest child can feel he is less competent. His brothers and sisters may enhance this self-perception by failing to take him seriously when he tries to express an idea. As a result of this experience, he may struggle to be acknowledged wherever he goes, his whole life long. If his brothers and sisters also react with jealousy when he shows his abilities, he may unfortunately learn to hold back or downplay his knowledge and talents around others.

As the youngest, she will feel left out when her brothers and sisters are old enough to go out in a rowboat alone but she must wait on the shore, or if her siblings try to ditch her. According to Molly, the six-year-old youngest of four, "Sometimes my sisters will tell me to stay where I am for five minutes. Then they run off, and never return." Usually the child above her in the birth order will give her the hardest time, because she is the most jealous of her. Amelia, the twenty-eight-year-old youngest sibling of eight, says, "To this day, my sister right above me puts my son and me down every chance she gets."

In some families, older siblings take out many of their frustrations on the youngest and can be very cruel to him, especially if they feel that Mom and Dad pamper him or if they are forced to care for him too much. As the littlest of many, he may even be held upside down by his ankles and sat upon.

Even though the youngest may have attained some skills to assert herself, when she comes up against her brothers and sisters, she can feel totally powerless. Out of sheer frustration, she may cry or throw a tantrum when she wants her sister to give her back her Barbie doll. If this behavior seems to help her, she may continue to use these tactics with others as she grows, often to the detriment of her relationships.

Helping Your Youngest Child to Grow

You will need to tune in to your youngest child and make sure that she is getting enough quality time. Try to read to her and enroll her in activities of her choice. It is important to caution her sisters and brothers about jumping in too quickly to take over for her and encourage her to work through problems on her own, instead. Make sure to set limits with your youngest and give her some responsibilities, too; even the smallest task will teach her to be responsible. Reassure your youngest that when she grows up, she will be able to do what her siblings can. Encourage her to express her ideas and insist that her siblings stop and listen respectfully, too. Intervene with your older children if they are acting too demeaning or physically aggressive toward her, and teach your youngest ways to assert herself.

If you make the rules equitable, if you avoid immediately siding with your youngest one when there is a quarrel and saddling the oldest ones with her care too much, the oldest children will resent her less and treat her more kindly.

Refer back to Chapter Three for important techniques to use to implement these approaches.

It is clear from the description of the children's lives and needs in each birth order position that raising a large family is harder than managing a small one. But if the parents can set a positive tone for family relationships and find ways to be emotionally present for each child, the children will benefit from all the positives a large family has to offer.

8

Close Together or Far Apart: Age Gap

"Oh! Let's just get it over with. We'll be finished with the diapers and bottles all at once." Many parents decide that having one baby right after another is the best route to go. Either they believe that their children will feel closer, they want to finish childrearing when they are young (and perhaps get back to their careers), or they have started having children later in life and simply cannot wait too long in between children. Other parents choose to have a large age span between their children, so that they can give each child more individualized attention. Large or small, these age differences will color the children's birth order experiences. This chapter will point out some of the benefits and challenges of either spacing and show you how you can be of help to your children.

Firstborn Children

While it is true that a firstborn child will have a reaction to the birth of a sibling at any age, many experts agree that the child tends to adjust more easily when there is a larger age gap between the two. If the firstborn child is from three to five years older, generally considered to be a good spacing, he will already be forming his own separate life. He may be out of the house several hours a day at nursery school or kindergarten, have friends and activities that he enjoys, and be less dependent upon his parents. Most importantly, he will have had several years of his parents' undivided attention and, therefore, feel a more secure bond with them.

An older child will be more capable of verbalizing her emotions, too. She might say, "I'm jealous," rather than biting her baby brother or throwing her blocks around the room. This will help her parents to help her. She will also grasp her parents' explanations better, such as "When you were little we diapered you and gave you bottles, too," and be able to play by herself when her parents are bathing the baby. Toddlers and even two-year-olds cannot. It is important to note that if the secondborn child comes only one or two years after the first, the parents' job will be harder, too. They will be raising two babies at the same time. Stressed out by the amount of work they have, the parents might find it very difficult to balance the needs of both their children.

Many other siblings seem to enjoy having a large age difference with their siblings. As Lyndsey, an eight-year-old with a brother four years younger, puts it, "I like being smarter than my brother. I can trick him and make him get up when he's sitting in my favorite chair, by telling him that another chair is better." She wishes her brother were even younger. "If he was younger, he might be less annoying and less of a tattletale." Most firstborns realize that the closer in age a younger sibling is, the more he would want to play with their toys and copy everything they do. Perhaps this is why when there are three children in a family, the oldest often expresses a preference for the youngest and tends to have a more tranquil relationship with her, too.

Some parents find that having their children very close in age makes them more compatible playmates. They have common interests and can understand each other better. One mother comments, "My oldest and youngest are only eighteen months apart, and they are best buddies. They spend hours in the brook out back hunting for tadpoles together and would rather play with each other than anyone else. If there were more years in between them, I don't know if they would be so close." Gabriel, the seven-year-old oldest brother of a five-and-a-half-year-old brother and a three-year-old sister, sees the benefit of having a sibling close in age to him. "My brother and I like watching sports on TV together. If he was little, he'd want me to switch to Barney, like my sister, and there would be too much Barney in this house." He adds, "My brother can aim and catch good so we can play baseball, too." Some adults will attest that because they grew up so close in age to their sibling, they have remained best friends throughout life.

However, it is also true that the smaller the age gap, the more competitive children can be. According to Seymour Reit in his book *Sibling Rivalry*, "Competition and rivalry between siblings is usually most intense when the kids are closer in age—where the span between them is three years or less." The two children have similar needs, and they are vying for the same kind of attention. That is why twins can be so highly competitive and why it is not unusual to see a toddler trying to pull his new baby sister off his mom's lap.

Sometimes a firstborn child with a sibling who is close in age can feel very shortchanged, especially if they are treated like twins. Because of their small age difference, they may be dressed alike and eventually end up playing on the same soccer team. This enhances not only their competitiveness but also their need to feel different. And if the secondborn child turns out to be more skilled than his sibling in kicking in a goal, the older one will feel diminished. One fifty-eight-year-old man recalls how upset he was as a youngster when his brother, only a year younger, was put into his kindergarten class. He still resents the fact that as they grew up, his brother was always right on his heels, horning in on his territory. The older child may feel especially angry, too, if he is required to help out in the house more than his eleven-month-younger sibling and even asked to baby-sit for him.

With a larger age gap, the oldest sibling tends to be more nurturing and less rivalrous toward his younger sibling. But there are some downsides to a large age difference, too. If the oldest is spaced far apart from the secondborn child, the two children may not have many common interests or abilities. Danielle, a little girl who is six years older than her younger sister, complains, "I can't even play board games with my sister. She can't read the instructions." However, even children who are many years apart in age seem to find ways to play together. Besides, as they get older, the age difference will diminish in importance.

If there are several children in the family, the oldest and the youngest ones can be as much as twenty years apart, and it will be hard for them to forge a connection. Reflecting upon the issue, Meredith, the fifteen-year-old oldest sister of three, says, "I simply cannot get into my seven-year-old younger brother's head, nor he in mine. We hardly spend any time together." An older child who does not have a sibling until he's eight will have the benefits of being raised as an only child, but can have a very rough time when he suddenly has to share the affections of his parents and his relatives for the first time.

Laterborns

Though the second child who is born soon after the firstborn will enjoy all the fun things he can do with his older sibling, he may have a harder time getting his parents' attention than if the two were more widely spaced. The parents may be so busy trying to get through the day and reassuring their older child (who may be acting out) that they still love him, that they are unable to spend much time alone with their younger one. In her book, *Your Second Child*, Joan Solomon Weiss quotes a study done by researchers Michael Lewis and Valerie S. Kreitzberg of the Educational Testing Service that supports the benefit of wider spacing for babies. "Babies born at least three and a half years after their next older siblings were looked at more, smiled at more, and played with more than babies who came along sooner.

The secondborn child will work hard to equal her older sibling and establish her own identity. But with a small age difference between the two, the second one may be more acutely aware that she is lagging behind. After all, they are almost the same age and size (the second child might even be bigger) so she should be able to do the same things. A thirty-five-year-old woman who is the secondborn of six recalls, "I was put in the same tap-dancing class as my sister a year and a day older than me. She was put in the front row, but I was placed in the back because I had trouble keeping up. Since then, I have always believed that I am uncoordinated." Because the secondborn child close in age poses such a threat to her older sibling's status, she will also have to put up with the older one constantly flaunting their age difference and bullying her.

The same pluses and minuses hold true for middle children, too. With several years between them, the second, third, or fourth child would be older and more capable of handling his or her displacement when the time came. They would also have more of an opportunity to reap the benefit of being the youngest. Nina, the third sister of four, five years older than her youngest sister, relates, "I was glad my youngest sister was born so much later. I got to be the baby for a long time."

If the children in the middle come one after the other, they will have a stronger rivalry and each one will have a harder time getting enough recognition. There might be three children in high school together, sharing the same teachers, the same circle of friends, and even competing for the same boyfriends and girlfriends.

In large families sometimes several children are born in a row and then there is a hiatus of several years before the next group of children. In such a case, a fourth child born three or more years after his older siblings can become like the oldest sibling to the next three. Large families tend to split up into small groups, depending upon the ages of the children. The children closest in age tend to spend the most time together, and even though they may be the most rivalrous, they can ironically be the closest. Francine Klagsbrun, in *Mixed Feelings*, remarks, "For many siblings, nearness in age generates conflict and competition that coexist with feelings of closeness."

And Along Came the Baby

If the youngest child is close in age to her siblings, she will have the benefit of palling around with them. If she arrives many years later, though, there will be other advantages. Paula, the six-year-old youngest sister of four, remarks, "If everyone was closer in age to me, they would need to hold Mommy's hand, too." When the baby is much younger, she may be doted upon by everyone in the family. Of course she may be simultaneously loved and envied for being the youngest.

With a huge age gap between the youngest and her siblings, the youngest child grows up like an only child. The thirty-year-old youngest brother of three observes, "Since I was born nine and twelve years apart from my two brothers, after the age of seven they were both in college, and I grew up alone. This age gap reduced any chance for competition or friction with my brothers."

If the youngest child is born at a time when the others are more or less grown, or the parents are feeling more financially secure and fulfilled with their lives, the child can benefit tremendously. She may receive more quality attention than the others did and even be the only one to go to college. But if her arrival is considered an extra burden or an intrusion in the parents' lives, she may unfortunately end up feeling unwanted instead.

Growing up spaced far apart from her sisters and brothers, the youngest can feel very lonely. With the older ones so caught up in their lives, or living far away from home, she may feel little or no connection to her siblings, and be forced to turn to her friends for companionship instead. Melissa, the youngest sister of three, spaced eight and ten years from her older siblings, says, "When I was little, I did not really have any relationship with my older siblings. Later on in life, our age differences meant less and we became very close."

Working with Your Children's Age Differences

Help each child deal with a dethronement. When you have a new baby, keep in mind that even your fully grown child will have some feelings of jealousy. It is natural. Therefore, it is wise to speak with all your children openly about their feelings and be accepting of their emotions. You will need to work hard with your older children to reassure them that they are still loved, while making sure to spend enough time with your baby.

Assist your children who are close in age in developing their individuality. If any two of your children are very close in age, try to help each one to develop his own unique interests and individuality. It is best to place them in separate classes at school and encourage them to find some of their own after-school activities and friendships. On the other hand, it is positive to support their shared interests, too. For example, they might enjoy attending a program about dinosaurs at the museum together. If your children are very competitive, provide them with an opportunity to talk about their feelings and give them support and reassurance that they are equally loved. Engaging them in cooperative activities, such as taking care of a pet hamster together and spending time alone with each, will help diminish their competition.

Involve your children who are spaced further apart in each other's lives. To bridge the gap between your siblings who are spaced far apart, involve your older child in your younger child's care (if he or she is willing). For example, a six-year-old might enjoy feeding his little sister. Help the two to find activities that they can share, too. An eleven-year-old and a six-year-old can play Nintendo games together or sit next to each other when they are doing their homework. The older one can help the younger one when he gets stuck. If your older child is grown, invite him to your younger one's school play, or ask him to teach his brother how to ride a two-wheeler.

It is apparent that large and small age differences can affect how siblings feel about each other and about themselves. A small age gap has the benefit of promoting closeness, but it also creates tremendous rivalry and identity problems for children. A larger age difference gives children more space to be individuals and have more of their parents' attention, but it can create distance between siblings. Ultimately, it is up to the parents to make the decision about how to space their children according to the needs of their family. But if parents provide their children with support and nurture their relationships in the ways suggested, the children can more easily overcome any of the challenges these age differences create.

Does Gender Matter?

"I got better grades than my younger brother did in high school. But when it came time for college, he was sent to an Ivy League school and I had to go to a community college," one forty-two-year-old woman laments.

A six-year-old boy complains, "My eight-year-old brother is in the gifted class at school. Everyone makes a big deal over him. But when I get a 100 on my spelling test, nobody seems to care."

A child's gender and the gender of his siblings will affect his daily experience in the family. Children with siblings of the opposite sex must cope with any disparities in their treatment. Same-sex siblings will have to compete hard to carve out their own special place in the family. This chapter will raise your awareness of the kinds of rivalries, resentments, and self-esteem problems that children face in their birth order positions as a result of these gender-related issues and will guide you in helping your children feel equally loved.

Firstborn Son

Since time immemorial, the birth of a firstborn son has been cause for celebration. This baby assured the family that there would be an heir. While crowns are rarely handed down in most families today, the oldest male child is often expected to carry on the family name and status.

Parents often convey to their firstborn son, through their words and actions, that he is "God's greatest gift to the world" but also that they expect the world of him. In many homes, it is assumed that he will follow in his father's footsteps. If Dad is a doctor, his son must become one, too (although sometimes a lawyer will do). If Dad played college football, his son must try out for the team. In some cases, Dad might insist that his son be groomed to run the family business. If Mom wished Dad could have been more successful, she might push her son to achieve more. These pressures can be greatest for a male only child.

In some cases, the oldest boy is expected to quit school and support his younger siblings when it is deemed necessary and take charge when there is a family crisis. And what happens if the son is either uninterested in Dad's choices, refuses to go along with the program, or simply folds under the pressure? He can face ridicule and emotional abandonment. In such a situation, the parents might turn to the son next in line (even if he is the youngest), or a daughter, to pick up the ball.

It is almost uncanny how some parents who desperately want their child to succeed interfere so much that they can actually prevent this from happening. Torn between doing what his parents want and what he wants to do, the child becomes totally paralyzed and unable to move ahead.

The firstborn son can feel very jealous and resentful if a daughter is born right after him and she receives preferential treatment. For example, he will get angry if his sister is excused from carrying the groceries in from the car because it is a "man's job," or if she always gets to pick a treat first because of the rule "ladies first." It will upset him tremendously if he is constantly criticized for his "boyish" behavior, such as being very active, and compared to his sister ("Why do you have to be so wild? Look how quietly your sister plays"). Steven, the seven-year-old brother of a younger sister, complains, "When my sister is mad, she will hit me and punch me and get away with it. But if I hit her back, I'm told, 'Boys are not supposed to hit girls,' and I am punished." These double standards may leave him feeling less loved. He will feel very confused, too, by the inconsistent messages he is receiving about his worth as a boy. It will be particularly difficult for him if his sister is allowed to follow her own path in life, while his parents are always trying to direct his.

Antiquated societal demands that boys must be brave, strong, and capable at all times so they can go out and bring home the bacon (like their primordial ancestors) still color the way parents socialize their children. Unfortunately, these tough standards cause boys to feel the need to be superhuman (so they cut off their emotions), to view themselves as failures when they perceive that they are not measuring up, and to become enraged with their parents for their lack of support. Luckily, there is a growing awareness that if parents pressure their sons less, encourage them to express their emotions, and teach them to be nurturers (not just breadwinners), they strengthen their sons and prepare them better for life.

It is important to note that a secondborn, middle, or youngest boy will face the same kind of gender-related issues with his older or younger sisters. If the firstborn child is followed by a boy, he will deal with other issues that will be discussed in the section on laterborns.

The Firstborn Daughter

If the firstborn child is a daughter, in many families she will be the one expected to carry forth the family banner. In some cases, a daughter may be particularly pressured to live out her mother's unfulfilled dreams. For example, if Mom married, stayed at home to raise a family and was unhappy, she may try to live vicariously through her daughter and pressure her to build a career:

her daughter must not live the same life that she did. Unfortunately, her mother's (or parents') interference can undo the firstborn daughter's success, just as it would for her male counterpart. All of these issues can be especially intense for a female only child.

If the firstborn daughter senses that her parent is deeply disappointed with her gender (which may be perceptible even when it is unspoken), she will feel inadequate and struggle her whole life to measure up. This can be particularly difficult for her if her birth followed the death or miscarriage of a son.

The firstborn daughter will have some additional stresses as she tries to succeed. At the same time that she is trying to accomplish her goals, she can face sex discrimination at school and in the workplace. She may struggle hard to gain recognition from teachers who favor boys, or to enter fields that are male-dominated. At times, she might also be hesitant to compete, because despite all of our societal advances, girls are still made to feel that being too aggressive is not feminine. At the heart of all these issues is the disturbing reality that in many ways girls are still looked upon and treated as second-class citizens in our society.

In many situations, especially in large families, the oldest daughter is expected to take on the role of the second caretaker of the family. Not only may there be a need for her to do so, but this role is also linked to her ancestral mandate as a woman to be the nurturer of the family. In some hard-pressed families, if Mom and Dad work long hours (or are divorced), the oldest daughter may be required to care for and supervise her siblings much of the day. Unfortunately, in such a case, a firstborn girl may see her primary job in life as the caretaker of others; she may grow up feeling that it is wrong or even selfish to go out into the world and build an independent life, despite all the encouragement that girls are receiving today. If the firstborn daughter does not live up to her parents' expectations or opts out, the parents will look to their next daughter in line.

If she has a younger brother and he is treated like the "crown prince," the firstborn daughter can feel very slighted. Her anger will be exacerbated if there are double standards for her and her brother's behavior. As a girl, she may be expected to be super-polite, neat, unselfish, and never ever belligerent, otherwise she will be reprimanded for not being ladylike. These demands will be hard enough for her to live with. But if she is yelled at for dirtying her outfit or refusing to clean her room, while her brother can do the same and people just say, "Boys will be boys," she will be enraged. Adding fuel to the fire, her brother may constantly attack her self-worth by ribbing her, "Boys are smarter than girls," or "You can't run fast. You're a girl."

As she grows, she will feel very hurt if her brother receives special privileges and opportunities. As a thirty-eight-year-old first-born woman relates, "I always felt that I was treated differently than my younger brothers. They were allowed to participate in religious studies and political debates with my father, but I was never included." Another firstborn woman recalls, "My younger brother and I were both great at baseball and football. But nobody ever asked me if I wanted to play on a team." Sometimes, when there are limited funds in a family, a boy will be the one chosen to go to college because the parents just assume that the daughter will be taken care of by a husband. Daughters in other birth order positions deal with the same kinds of issues with their older and younger brothers.

Life can be hard for a daughter if she faces overly demanding expectations and frequent disparities in her treatment. As she grows, she may become highly self-critical whenever she senses that she is not living up to the standards for being "a good little girl" and often feel forced to repress her needs and her feelings, especially her anger, to fit into this ideal image. Any negative experiences that she has had in the family can leave her feeling less capable and loved than her brother, and even doubting her worth as a girl. These issues can plague her for her whole life.

As she grows, a daughter will face other societal pressures made upon women: to be pretty, thin, the perennial nurturer, and a perfect homemaker. And, if she chooses a career, she must be a superwoman who can manage both her home and her career perfectly.

Laterborns

Firstborns and their secondborn sisters and brothers who are of the same sex can be very competitive. According to Seymour Reit in *Sibling Rivalry*, "Surveys indicate there's more jealousy between same sex siblings than those of the opposite sex. Two children of the same sex close in age will have a lot of common needs and interests and they generate more quarrels and conflicts."

The secondborn child tries hard to catch up to the older one and establish his own identity. The older child feels very threatened with a same-sex sibling right below, who he fears might easily replace him, so he tries hard to keep his sibling in his place. Jonah, a seventeen-year-old secondborn son, talks about his early competition with his older brother: "When my brother and I were very little and we would have running races, I used to try my hardest, but he would always beat me. Whenever I would start to catch up, he would stick out his foot and trip me." Imagine how hard it would be for two sisters who were both trying out for the same leading role in their ballet recital.

If the firstborn child is a superstar in any way, or has an intensely close relationship with the parents, the second child of the same gender will have a harder time making her mark. In an attempt to try and grab some of the attention away, some secondborns can become supercompetitive with their older siblings while others may resort to negative behavior.

Middle children of three, four, or five same-sex siblings will also have a harder time gaining recognition. While the oldest and the youngest will have specified identities, the rest of the children must scramble to make a statement. And though there will be competition between any pair of same-sex siblings in the middle, adjacent children will usually be the most rivalrous.

A middle child who is the only one of his sex, however, will find it easier to differentiate himself. According to Bill, a twenty-eight-year-old man growing up with five sisters as the second youngest child, "My sisters were always grouped together, but I was special. When we entered a room we were announced thusly, 'Here are the Monahan sisters and Bill.' I felt I had an identity. It was easier for people to know me."

As the child who differs, he will probably receive many special privileges, too. He may have his own toys, his own room, and no hand-me-downs. His siblings may cherish him and look out for him, too. Bill, the man with five sisters, remembers, "The house-keeper called me the King."

The only boy or girl middle child will have his or her own challenges, though. As noted previously, this child may end up taking on the role of a firstborn boy or girl with all of its potential pressures. One secondborn daughter with five brothers who became the second mother of the family complains, "I lost my childhood taking care of my brothers."

The only boy or girl may also feel different at times. At certain ages a girl may tire of always roughhousing or playing with action figures. A boy may get bored playing house or dressing Barbie dolls. The opposite-sex sibling may enjoy having his or her room, but also feel left out and distant from the other children. During adolescence when the child is developing so differently, these feelings can be enhanced.

There are some very positive outcomes for a boy who grows up with sisters or a girl who grows up with brothers, however. If they have a good experience, such children tend to feel very comfortable with members of the opposite sex. They may even form close friendships with them, and end up marrying early and happily. An only boy or girl may even adopt some of the strengths of their opposite-sex siblings. For example, a girl may become more active and adventurous like her brothers, and a boy may develop his sister's sensitivity and understanding.

A child who lives with siblings of both sexes will have the benefit of learning how to get along with both. But he or she also faces all the complexities involved. Cindy, a forty-year-old woman, recalls some of the experiences she had as a middle sister of a brother and a sister. "When I was little, I mostly played dolls with my older sister, but I also liked playing sports with my younger brother and his friends. As I got older, though, I often felt like I didn't fit in with either sibling. My older sister and I fought a lot and she was into boys. Once I was too old to play football with the boys (I had started to develop, physically), I felt distant from my brother, too."

The Prince or Princess

The youngest boy of all brothers and the youngest girl of all sisters will receive much love and admiration from the family as the baby. But they will face some of their own challenges. Sometimes the youngest child can end up feeling that she got the short end of the stick. One thirty-eight-year-old woman, the youngest of four sisters, tells of a family party dress that got passed down from sister to sister: "By the time it got to me, it was quite faded."

In some cases, the youngest girl or boy may sense that with the last child, the family was hoping for a child of the opposite sex and feel that he or she is a disappointment to the family. As the youngest of three brothers, thirty-three-year-old Ralph recalls, "I knew I was supposed to be a girl." Parents need to monitor what friends and relatives say around their child ("Are you going to keep trying for that boy?") and the messages they themselves convey.

The youngest brother of sisters may be mothered by everyone. They may carry him around, dress him up, and do all his chores for him. His sisters might find their youngest brother useful, too. One youngest boy relates, "My sisters used to send me over to get

friendly with some boys they liked who lived down the block."
Sometimes, though, the youngest boy may receive special treatment from his parents, making his sisters resentful. The twenty-
nine-year-old younger brother of four sisters admits, "In high school,
if my sisters stayed out late and didn't call, my parents might
ground them for a week. But if I did the same, my parents would
just reprimand me."

The youngest girl of boys can be very special to her brothers,
too. An older brother may stick up for her when she is in trouble and even act as a father figure to her during a family crisis.
However, her brothers may be very jealous of her, too. She will
be the one who gets the huge dollhouse that is specially wired
by Dad or goes off for the afternoon with Mom to get her
nails done.

But in some ways the youngest girl is in double jeopardy.
Because she is both the tiniest and a girl, and boys are usually more
dominant and aggressive, they may speak for her, boss her around,
and even become physically aggressive with her.

Karli, a thirty-eight-year-old woman, recalls, "My two older
brothers picked on me because I was the weakest one. They used
to put me on their feet and catapult me across the room. They were
into James Bond, too, and they would pin me down and try out
new pressure points on me. I didn't think I would live to grow up."
Often parents are unaware of the level of aggression that may be
going on or how powerless their daughter feels. They really need to
be hypervigilant.

Because the youngest girl loves her brothers and wants to be just
like them, she may want to have her hair cut short and join in on
their baseball and hockey games. But they might tease her—"You
throw like a girl"—or refuse to let her play. As a result, she may
grow up feeling less capable than they and even angry about being
a girl.

Ironically, being the youngest girl in a family of boys can make
a girl tough. She is generally more involved in physical activities

because of her brothers and has learned early on that to survive, she must stand up for herself. As a result, she may be more fearless and self-confident than other girls.

In some cultures, the youngest daughter faces a unique challenge: her parents may expect her to be the one to stay home and take care of them in their old age and may try to hold her back from separating from the family.

Working with These Gender-Related Issues

Help your children to feel equally loved. There are many things you can do to help your children feel good about themselves and diminish their gender-related problems. First and foremost, you must help each child to feel equally loved and special. If you have one son and one daughter, they will automatically have their own uniqueness, but your same-sex children will need some extra help in developing theirs.

Treat your same-sex children as individuals. Praising each for her abilities and assisting them to explore their interests will help each child build a positive sense of self. When you can, try to give each of your children some time alone with you. Whether you plan a special breakfast out together or chat with her alone as you set the dinner table, this is by far the best way to communicate that she is important.

Help diminish your children's rivalry. To cut down on the rivalry so common to same-sex siblings, avoid using statements such as "Why can't you be as good a student as your older brother," or "Our secondborn is the pretty one." Whenever possible, try to give all of your same-sex children their own new toys and clothing, too, rather than strictly hand-me-downs. Keep every arena open to all of your children. Even if one child is a baseball superstar, the others should be allowed to join a team. Most importantly, avoid favoritism at all costs. It will cause the others to feel unloved.

Be equally respectful of your sons and your daughters. Since the gender issue is so complex in our society, there are many important approaches that you will need to take to help your sons and your daughters feel comfortable. Always try to be equally respectful toward both the boys and the girls and teach them to respect each other. Avoid comparing them or making statements that will diminish each one's pride in his or her own sex.

Treat your sons and your daughters according to the same standards. Like your sons, your daughters should be able to join a softball team and should not be allowed to hit others. Like your daughters, your sons should get a turn to pick their treat first and have an equal share in household responsibilities. Listen to your sons' and daughters' complaints when they feel they are being treated unfairly. There is often a valid point to consider. Encourage your sons to express their emotions and be supportive of them when they do. Acknowledge your daughters' right to feel angry, to be independent, and to be competitive.

Give both your sons and your daughters the message that they are capable of accomplishing big things. Praise your daughters for their intelligence and for what they accomplish, not just for how they look. Praise your sons for their humane qualities, not just their achievements. Try not to force your sons and daughters to live out your unfulfilled dreams or to discourage your child from choosing a career that is usually pursued by the opposite sex. Support your child's own path instead (unless it is self-destructive, of course), and you may be especially pleased by the outcome.

Teach your daughters to be assertive. You need to teach all of your children how to assert themselves, but your daughters may need some extra help. It is important that you make sure that your daughters get the opportunity to state their opinions and ask for what they want. You must step in and stop any verbal put-downs or physical aggression toward your daughters (and vice versa). Teach your daughters how to stand up for their rights. Support your daughters' (and your sons') inclusion in their siblings' activities, especially if they are the only child of the opposite sex. Rather than being too restrictive of your daughter and curtailing her freedom, teach her important coping skills, such as how to deal with strangers. You might also consider enrolling her in self-empowerment programs, such as a karate class, so she will feel strong and learn how to handle herself in the world.

Monitor your children's environment. Try to be aware of the kinds of messages your children are receiving about their sex in their environment. If you hear about any behaviors that are prejudicial against either boys or girls in your children's classes, try to intervene with your school. Monitor your children's TV viewing and point out any sexist remarks or interactions. Then discuss what is wrong with them.

Expose your children to positive role models. Read books with your children about important women in history who were strong and ambitious and men who were humanitarians and made valuable contributions to society. If you are working, allow your daughters and sons to spend a day at work with you so that they can see successful role models in action and learn to value each sex. Keep in mind that the way you treat your sons and daughters and the way you interact with your spouse or other adults of the opposite sex will become the most powerful model for how they will treat each other and how they will feel about their own sex.

Even though there is a greater awareness today of the damage that societal stereotypes and disparities in the treatment of boys and girls can do to the emotional well-being of children, old patterns are slow to change. However, you can actively make a difference in your own home by conveying love and acceptance to your sons and daughters and by treating them equally. This will ease any resentments or inadequacy that they might feel, as well as the added challenges these emotions pose to their birth order positions. What is essential here is that you concentrate on raising confident, sensitive, happy *people* and focus less on their gender.

Parental
Birth Order:
Making
Connections

🪲 *"Stop that!" six-year-old Megan screeches. Standing within earshot of this latest sibling squabble, Mom instantaneously calls out to her eight-year-old son, "Ben! You're punished!"*

Why is this mother so quick to lash out at her son? Maybe she is nervous because she is rushing to get the kids off to school on time, is worried about a car payment she has to make, or has a headache. Maybe this is already her children's tenth fight of the morning and she expects her oldest to behave better. But there is another possibility: Mom's reaction may be unconsciously determined by her early childhood relationships.

Among the current generation of parents, there is a growing awareness of the powerful influence of each individual's upbringing upon their relationships with their own children. For example, being raised by an authoritarian parent who doled out harsh punishment or one who was emotionally unavailable will often govern how the adult will react when her own child spills some milk, or asks for a new toy. She may repeat the same behavior or try to do the opposite. A parent may also project some of her feelings about her own parent onto her child. When dealing with a child who is not paying attention, the parent may relive the anguish she felt when relating to her own perennially distracted parent and over-react from frustration. Such projections are part of the parent-child relationship. Today, parents are trying hard to uncover the sources of their reactions, either on their own or with the help of a therapist, so that they can respond more appropriately to their children. The insights they are gaining are helping parents to stop themselves before they engage in negative behaviors that can harm their child's self-esteem or the parent-child relationship.

But there is another early relationship, often overlooked, that consciously or unconsciously colors the way a parent relates to his children: the sibling relationship. All the feelings of love, admiration, jealousy, anger, and resentment that the parent felt toward his siblings, connected to his birth order position, are projected onto his children and affect tremendously how he relates to them. The manner in which his parents treated him in his particular spot in the family will also shape his interactions with his children. For example, if, as a firstborn child, the parent was highly pressured to achieve, it will affect the kinds of demands he makes upon his own children. He might push them just as hard, or try to make their experience different by taking a more relaxed approach. If a parent was a secondborn child who was constantly criticized by his older sibling, this experience will govern how he reacts when his children start putting each other down.

It is evident that parents' birth order experiences powerfully impact their relationship with their children, and in this chapter we will see how. According to Donald and Lois Richardson in *Birth Order and You*, "Birth order explains why parents may treat each of their children differently. Their birth order can affect what they think of—and how they raise each of their children."

As we shall see, a parent may unconsciously identify with a child of the same birth order position because he reminds her of herself, and this identification may either soften her approach toward him or cause her to react more harshly. She may feel affectionate toward a child from another birth order position, or battle hard with him because of old unresolved feelings of jealousy and anger toward a sibling. Megan's mother in our anecdote is a good example of what can happen. Suppose she was a secondborn sibling with an older brother who often bullied her. When she lashes out at her son, she may unconsciously be venting her rage at her older brother and trying to protect her younger daughter, with whom she identifies.

It is very important to understand why many of these reactions occur unconsciously. It is the key to understanding oneself. In an attempt to cope with painful experiences, such as the birth of her sibling or the time her older sister got a brand-new dress for a wedding while she had to wear a hand-me-down, and the jealousy, rage, and guilt associated with them, the child employs various psychological protective maneuvers. These are called defense mechanisms and are designed to push painful thoughts, memories, and emotions out of conscious awareness. For example, an individual may employ denial, a refusal to acknowledge her emotions ("I never felt jealous of my brother"); repression, which involves pushing emotions down into the unconscious mind ("I have no memory of my sister's birth"); and reaction formation, a mechanism whereby the individual says and does the opposite of what she really feels ("I just love my new baby sister to death").

Not only do these defensive maneuvers help keep the pain away, but the whole process serves another purpose as well. Every child wants to be a good child who is valued and loved by her parents. Early on, she learns from her parents' reactions and from watching TV and the movies that in order for her to be considered a good child, she must not have or display any negative feelings toward her parents or her siblings. Therefore, she tries to have only loving feelings. But in reality, mixed feelings are a natural part of every relationship. So what's a little child to do? Dr. Jane Greer, in her book *Adult Sibling Rivalry*, describes this dilemma extremely well: "Emotions you feel are often exact opposites of each other. You love your brother but you hate him. You feel compassion for your sister, but you feel contempt as well. You feel nurturant toward your siblings but simultaneously desire to reject them." She continues, "To complicate matters, our culture places a strong emphasis on feeling pure emotions. Love, for instance, should be undiluted by selfishness, envy, fatigue, or impatience, much less polluted by anger and hate."

Gloria, a fifty-year-old woman, the younger of two sisters, recalls a very painful experience from childhood that demonstrates how hard it is for a child to cope with her emotions. "When I was eight years old, I was at my older sister's tenth birthday party and I was very jealous about all the attention and presents she was receiving. I felt left out and unloved. Finally, unable to bear the pain alone anymore, I turned to my grandmother, whom I felt close to at the time, and told her, 'Grandma, I feel so jealous of my sister.' My grandmother's face became twisted and she lashed out at me, 'That's disgusting.' That was the last time I openly showed this emotion."

Though this grandmother's response was particularly harsh, parents and other adults make statements such as "Don't be so selfish," or "You are an unkind brother" all the time when admonishing children for not wishing to share a toy or fighting over who gets to ride in the front seat of the car. And children end up feeling very guilty for their natural instincts. A similar outcome occurs when a child pushes a sibling who has just pinched him, beat him in a running race, or whom he feels is being favored by his parents. If he ends up being ridiculed and banished to his room, the child may conclude that jealousy and anger toward a sibling are bad. Children need understanding, limits, and coping skills, not guilt.

As she grows, the girl internalizes her parents' (and other adults') words so that, even in their absence, each time that she experiences these angry, jealous, or competitive feelings toward her siblings and others, her self-esteem drops. "There is a kind of shame in seeing oneself as competitive, someone who compares personal achievements or finances with those of another and who by implication may feel envious of the other. The shame is compounded when the other is a sibling whom we have been taught to love and protect," says Francine Klagsbrun in her tremendously insightful book, *Mixed Feelings.*

Out of troubling guilt and a wish to be loved, therefore, the individual will try to bury these feelings. This process can be so quick that the individual never even identifies them. Unfortunately, she may go through life trying desperately to hide her emotions and fearful of being found out. But this takes a tremendous amount of psychic energy, and often leaves the person feeling very anxious. Besides, repression is not foolproof. The feelings still rattle around inside, periodically breaking into consciousness and causing the individual pain.

If someone had been there to tell that eight-year-old at her sister's party that all children have jealous feelings, reassured her that she was equally loved, and found ways to include her rather than shaming her, her feelings would have remained in consciousness where she could manage them better. Her self-esteem would be intact, too. And so these memories of feeling left out, less loved by a parent, and even physically abused by a sibling remain tucked away as the child grows. But as soon as something occurs with her own children that looks or feels similar to her early sibling experiences, the old anger and jealousy can sudden reemerge.

Says one mother who is a secondborn sibling, "As soon as my daughter teases her younger sister the way my older brother teased me, I go right back to that child place. I become the baby who's being picked on and I react out of a place of instinct."

When the Parent and the Child Have the Same Birth Order Position

As we have seen, a parent can strongly identify with the child who is in the same birth order position as she is. If the child is the same sex or temperament as the parent, this identification will undoubtedly be more intense. Annette, a firstborn daughter with a second-born brother who is the mother of a firstborn daughter and a secondborn son, mirroring her own sibling relationship, talks about this experience: "There is more of a kindred spirit between me and my daughter. I can easily get what her frustrations are about having a younger brother. I have been there myself." Jerry, who is the secondborn of two brothers, says, "I feel I understand what my younger son is going through more. He's very much like me. He even looks like me." If the child carries the same name as the parent, the association will be strengthened.

At first glance, this identification may not be apparent to some parents, especially when the child who is in the same birth order position seems to have a totally different personality. For example, if as a youngest sibling a mother was shy and withdrawn but her own youngest daughter is outgoing and assertive, it may be hard for the mother to see any similarity between them, apart from their gender. But, after some reflection, like other parents she will usually be able to point to some situations that actually do spark a birth order identification for her. For example, when her older children refuse to let her daughter join in on their play or they ridicule her ideas, she can feel her blood pressure rising.

A parent can also identify with a child of the opposite sex if he is occupying the identical birth order position. Abby, a secondborn sibling who has an older daughter and a younger son, says, "I identify with James when Maddie is using her superior intelligence to harass him." Lisa, the middle sister between two brothers, strongly identifies with her middle son, who has an older and a younger sister. "I identify with Patrick as the one in the middle who is the odd one out."

A strong parental identification can affect a child very positively. The parent may be more sensitive to the child's issues. Says one firstborn father of two, "I feel very sympathetic to my older child so I can help him with his frustrations. Sometimes I'll tell him, 'It's hard to have a younger brother who wants to be part of everything you do and always gets into your stuff.' " One secondborn mother works hard with her secondborn daughter to prevent her from feeling inferior to her older brother by constantly praising her and encouraging her. At an extreme, a parent might end up favoring this child and set him apart from his siblings.

However, an intense identification with a child can bring up very painful feelings for the parent. The parent may often feel anxious and worried for the child. Claire, a firstborn mother, recalls how upset she felt when she was pregnant with her second child: "I was literally grieving for my oldest daughter, Sara. I knew it was going to be difficult for her. I felt my own sadness, too. I thought to myself, 'I'm never going to have pizza alone with her again.' "

When watching her six-year-old daughter acting highly critical of her newly acquired writing skills, the firstborn mother of two daughters worried that her child was growing up to be a perfectionist like herself. Unfortunately, her overidentification with her daughter was probably blurring this mother's vision and causing her unnecessary pain. If no one was causing her undue stress, the child was probably just going through a natural developmental phase. When children first learn to write in school, they commonly try to write their letters perfectly and can easily feel exasperated. Parents often make these "parental leaps" when they project their own personal issues onto a situation.

In the best-case scenario, when parents reexperience their own early childhood pain in this way, they can use their deeper understanding to extend extra support to the child and assist him in working through his problems. But sometimes, the parent may feel so hysterical that she communicates her anxiety to the child. She might feel utterly powerless to help him, too. After all, she could not help herself when she had a similar problem as a child. She may even continue to struggle with the same issue as an adult. In the end, the child will be left to deal with the problem on his own.

Sometimes, a parent can have a negative identification with his child. If the parent sees what appears to be an aspect of himself in his child that he does not like, he may get angry and behave negatively. Says one firstborn mother, "Whenever I see my older daughter hurting her younger brother, I see her as a reflection of myself. I feel guilty about the way I mistreated my younger sibling and I start screaming." One secondborn father becomes enraged with his secondborn son every time he gives up when he is trying something new. Realizing the source of his anger, he admits, "I often felt inadequate in relation to my older brother and would stop trying. I don't want my son to be a quitter too." As we can see, fear and guilt are often behind parental anger.

Another even more complicated process can occur, called identification with the aggressor. This happens in more severe cases in which a person has been treated especially badly by a sibling or a parent. According to Francine Klagsbrun in *Mixed Feelings*, "They [the parents] see themselves as the other saw them, weak, slow or otherwise inadequate. They then project that poor image of themselves onto a child who resembles them in birth order, gender, or temperament." The parent then behaves toward the child according to how he or she was treated. For example, a father who grew up with an abusive older brother, who constantly called him "dumb" and frequently punched him whenever he made a mistake, might chastise his secondborn son when he accidentally knocks over a vase, and even spank him.

Unfortunately, the parental rejection that the child experiences from these negative types of identification can have grave consequences. Ignorant of what is really bothering the parent, the child can easily conclude that he is no good.

When the Parent and Child Have
Different Birth Order Positions

Parents often find it somewhat harder to comprehend the experience of a child in a different birth order position from their own. Says Stephanie, one firstborn mother, "It's less natural for me to put myself in my younger son's shoes, but it's enlightening for me to see what happens for him. It helps me to see what life was like for my younger brother." Here is one of her insights: "Life was so simple for my daughter, Katie. Everything she did was wonderful and we told her so. Who was to say different? But when Joey draws a cat and I tell him it's wonderful, he's no dummy. He sees his cat doesn't look like Katie's, so he knows he doesn't measure up." Her deeper understanding of her son is helping her to be more empathetic toward her younger brother, and to build a better relationship with him.

Nevertheless, a parent can, in fact, identify with a child in another birth order position if that child is of the same gender or has a similar temperament to the parent. Julia, one secondborn mother, realizes that because she had an abusive older brother, she alternates between identifying with her secondborn son (because of his birth order position) when he is being put down by his older sister, and identifying with her daughter (because of her gender) when the younger one retaliates physically. One firstborn father says he can easily relate to his youngest son who, like him, is shy around people.

Parents can also unconsciously relate to their children in other birth order positions as if they were their siblings. Dr. Jane Greer, in *Adult Sibling Rivalry*, uses an extremely valuable term, the "invisible sibling," that can help one understand exactly what happens. According to Dr. Greer, an "invisible sibling" is "someone other than a sibling whose presence in your life evokes feelings of siblinghood, some of which may be positive (love, admiration, appreciation) and some negative (dislike, hatred, contempt)." The invisible sibling can take on the form of a boss, best friend, or child, and, as Dr. Greer phrases it, "in a sense you are boxing with shadows." Here, we will see how an invisible sibling affects the parent-child relationship.

Sometimes an adult will transfer the affection she felt toward a sibling to her child. Janet, the oldest sister of two brothers, with two grown sons of her own, talks about her loving feelings toward her youngest child. "He reminds me of William, my youngest brother, whom I loved and treated like my baby doll." She realizes that at times she reacts more kindly to him than to her older son, who reminds her of her middle brother, with whom she was always fiercely competitive.

But an interaction between one's own children can also ignite the old rage a parent felt toward a sibling. "I get furious with my older son whenever he intellectually bulldozes my younger son," relates Audrey, a secondborn parent. Debbie, the middle child of three, says, "Whenever my older daughter fake-hits my middle son, I freak. My older brother used to do that to me, and I never knew when he would actually connect."

However, even when the child is not really misbehaving, the parent may be so sensitive to an issue that she may misread the situation. Many of these unconscious associations cause parents to label the child who reminds them of their sibling the "bad child" or to scream at, tease, and act punitively toward him. It is important to note that frequently the parent's underlying anger really has to do with some unresolved anger toward one of her own parents, who may have given her a hard time. But since children need their parents so badly, they often find it safer to direct their anger toward a sibling. Therefore, an adult might feel jealous toward a brother or sister who got more attention, rather than blaming his parent for not making sure that everyone got enough.

Interestingly enough, sometimes a parent can identify with a child from another birth order position and view the child who occupies her own spot as her invisible sibling. For example, one middleborn father sides with his middleborn daughter when his youngest son provokes her. But he stands firmly behind his youngest son when his daughter bosses him around, because she reminds him of his domineering older sister.

In many circumstances, a parent can actually play out some unresolved birth order issues with her own children as if they were her siblings. A firstborn husband may feel jealous when his child is born and compete with him for his wife's affection. Later on in life, he may even try to beat him on the tennis court. A secondborn parent's unresolved need to be number one can conflict with her loving wishes for her child. She may become ecstatic when he is applying to an Ivy League college, but because of the envious feelings toward her older brother left over from childhood, she may unconsciously behave in ways that undermine his attempts.

Most parents consciously or unconsciously set out to repair what happened to them in their families of origin. Carol, the youngest child of three, openly admits, "My upbringing has set me on a path to correcting all the wrongs that were done to me." Having grown up as the youngest sister of two verbally abusive older brothers, she will not allow her own sons to say mean things to her youngest daughter. She watches, listens, and intervenes to protect her. Says she, "The abusive words stick with you for a lifetime," and she wants to prevent this from happening.

Brian, the oldest brother of four children, is extra kind to his secondborn child, because he is trying hard to make up for the rageful feelings and behavior he had toward his secondborn brother. Rebecca, a firstborn twin, who was as highly pressured as any firstborn child and felt she was always "glommed together with her identical twin," works hard to make her own twins' experience different from her own. She is careful to give each child some individual time, helps each develop a separate identity, and minimizes the importance of their age difference whenever it comes up.

As the parent intervenes to create a more positive experience for his children, he can undergo an internal reparative process, too. If he helps his younger child assert himself with an older sibling, something he could never do, he can feel stronger and may be able to use the same skill with others. If he intervenes in a sibling battle to prevent his children from hurting each other, he may fulfill an unresolved wish that his own parent had stepped in to protect him. He will experience vicarious pleasure, too, as he helps his children to achieve a kind, loving relationship that is closer to the ideal sibling relationship that he always dreamed of.

In an effort to correct what happened to them, parents often determine the number of children that they will have according to their birth order experience. A parent who is an only child may go to great lengths to have a second child because she does not want her child to feel the loneliness that she did. A younger sibling who felt her older sibling was preferred might decide to have only one child, because she wants him to reap the benefits of being the center of attention, or because she does not wish to reexperience the pain of her own sibling relationship via her children.

Now comes the clincher. There are usually two parents simultaneously playing out with their children their unresolved jealousy, anger, and resentment from their sibling relationships. This can cause complications for everyone. With two adults in the picture, there are many possible scenarios that can occur in regard to birth order. Sometimes the two parents may come from the same birth order position and act in concert. If they are both firstborn children, for example, they may each identify with their older child and support him when he fails a math test. But it is also possible that both parents may come down hard on him. If they have been raised to be perfectionists, they might want him to be perfect, too. At the same time, they may favor their younger child, with whom they identify less strongly. If both parents frequently line up against their older child, life will be extremely difficult for him. However, sometimes one of these firstborn parents might be hard on the child, while the other parent tries to treat him gently, out of a desire to repair her own early childhood experience. In this case, the two parents may end up in constant disagreement.

Two parents from different birth order positions may act in accord, too, but sometimes for different reasons. For example, a wife who is a secondborn child may get angry at her daughter, the youngest of four, when she refuses to dress herself. This behavior reminds her of her own dependency, which she disdains. Her husband, the third of four siblings, may find himself yelling at his youngest daughter too, because to him she symbolically represents his own youngest sister, who displaced him and received much attention as the helpless baby. Here, too, the child is in a very tough position.

But, sometimes, especially in two-child families, the mother and father each side with a different child along birth order lines. For example, identifying with his firstborn daughter, a firstborn husband may say of her, "Caitlin should never be punished. She never does anything wrong," while his secondborn wife may feel more inclined to side with their younger son. This split can lead to unfortunate alliances between the parents and children, leaving each child feeling unloved by one parent.

Spousal behaviors such as consistently picking on one child, favoring another, teasing, yelling, or hitting can cause harm to children and lead to severe marital strife. That is why it is crucial for parents to analyze their own reactions, discuss them with each other, and work together to choose the healthiest responses.

Working with Your Birth Order Issues

Self-analysis is the key. It is clear from our discussion that a parent's birth order experience powerfully affects the parent-child relationship. And since many of the connections between the past and the present are made unconsciously, it is crucial that you try and bring these issues into awareness. It is only then that you will be able to understand what you are dealing with and respond more objectively to your child. For example, Megan's mother in our opening anecdote needs to see that she is actually yelling at her brother, not just at her son, because she is trying to rectify what happened to her as a little girl. Once she identifies the source of her reaction, she could pull back to a more objective position. Rather than immediately blaming her son, she might clarify what happened.

Identify your strong emotions. How can you as a parent accomplish this important goal? When you find yourself getting extremely upset by one of your children's behaviors, such as your older child teasing your younger child, try to slow things down before you overreact. Strong feelings are often a sign that you are having a personal reaction to your child, especially if they seem out of proportion to what is actually going on. Consistently siding with one child or battling with another is also a definite giveaway. Something is up. Take a deep breath, count to ten, or walk out of the room for a few moments to gain your composure. Unless something harmful is happening, you do not have to react immediately. Ask yourself some quick questions: What am I feeling? Anger? Jealousy? Resentment? Who does this child remind me of right now? My sister? My father? My spouse? Myself? Did something like this ever happen to me when I was small?

Finding the answers may not be easy. As we discussed earlier in this chapter, feelings can be extremely painful and hard to look at. For example, acknowledging that you are jealous of your child might seem so shameful to you that you might try to hide it. But this acknowledgment is crucial for coping with the emotion and behaving more appropriately with your child. Therefore, try to be as accepting and supportive of your own feelings as you would be of your child's emotions.

Connect your feelings to a past experience. If you can connect your feelings to a real-life experience from the past, you will feel tremendous relief. For example, if you can determine that you feel jealous of your daughter when your husband is reading her a story, because at such moments she reminds you of your older sister who received more attention from your mother than you did, you will be on the right track. If you explain to yourself further that this early experience has made it hard for you to share the people you love, you will be far more forgiving of your emotion. You are not bad. Your feeling comes from a real experience that you had. When difficult feelings arise, it would be extremely helpful for you to repeat these phrases to yourself. The more specific you can get, the better. For example, remember the time your mother chatted with your sister and not to you when the three of you lay on chaise longues at the beach. Comparing the way you felt then with the way you feel now will help you understand what you are experiencing.

Once you can label your emotions and identify their source, you will immediately start to feel better. Having a framework for feelings makes them seem much more manageable. Next, allow yourself to feel angry at the real perpetrator. In one situation it might be your parent for not making sure to give you equal attention. In another, you might be mad at your brother for always teasing you. You will feel less angry at your child.

Work on your negative identifications with your child. If the source of your emotional distress is that you have identified what appears to be an intolerable aspect of yourself in your child—for example, your habit of procrastination—there are some steps that you can take. First and foremost, you must recognize that you and he are not the same person. You are two separate people with your own set of feelings and experiences. And besides, he has you to help him manage life better. Try to read all that you can, talk with other parents, and attend parenting workshops, so that you can learn which of your child's behaviors are purely developmental. This way you will project your own experiences onto his behavior less and understand him better. You might discover that your child is delaying getting ready for bed every night because going to sleep means a separation from you and the world he loves. This is not a reflection upon you.

All of these measures should help you establish a greater psychological distance from your child and enable you to respond to him more objectively. Keep in mind that in the beginning making connections between your emotions and your behavior will not be simple. You may not be able to understand what has happened during an incident until after you have exploded at your child, maybe even several days later. But the more you think about situations in this way, the more accessible the answers will become.

Get some support. Clarifying how your early childhood affects you can be difficult. You might find that talking about your emotions with a supportive spouse or a friend can give you important insights. However, if you feel you need more assistance, you might consider seeing a professional.

Raise your awareness of your birth order experience. Raising your consciousness about your early birth order experience will help this process along. It can help you figure out why you are always teasing your child or why you flare up at her so intensely when she will not share her toys. To begin with, you might reread the chapter pertaining to your specific place in the birth order. See if you can recall any of the feelings described and try to think about how your current behaviors are related.

Take a look at the explanations and suggestions included in each chapter that are recommended for use with your child. These are designed to soothe your child by giving him an emotional framework for what he is experiencing. They also relieve guilt. There are reasons for her feelings, and they are natural and acceptable. The specific suggestions offered are concrete steps to take to help her cope.

When self-administered, these approaches can help you, too! For example, if you as a firstborn child suffer because you are extremely hard on yourself and your children, you will begin to feel better if you can explain the reason why. Your parents were inexperienced and were very anxious about doing a good job. If you succeeded at something you were doing, they were reassured that things were going well. That is why they were so tough on you—not because you were not good enough. So, in essence, you are treating yourself the way they treated you. To feel better you must try to readjust your standards. You cannot be perfect, nor do

you have to be in order to be loved. Drop your harsh self-criticisms
and compliment yourself frequently, instead. Once you are kinder
to yourself, you will ease up on your child, too.

If it is clear to you that as the secondborn child in your family,
you have always felt inferior to your older sibling, try this. When
the feeling arises, remind yourself that this feeling began because
of the age difference between you and your older sibling. You
could not have had the same abilities then, but you do now. Take
stock of all your accomplishments and try hard not to compare
yourself to your sibling.

Reread the chapter on your sibling's birth order position. Now
that you have read about your own birth order experience, you
might try reading about your sibling's. It will give you even more
clarity about yourself and may improve your relationship. Understanding that your older sibling rejected you because it was hard
for him to share his parents with you will reinforce the reality that
you were not to blame. You might even feel more forgiving of him
and find it easier to spend time with him.

Try to talk over old issues with your sibling. Some adults take
another step in an effort to resolve their birth order issues and
strengthen their sibling relationship: they try to communicate with
their siblings about their past and current relationship. If you can
work through some old anger or jealousies with your siblings, these
emotions will be less likely to spill over into your relationship with
your child. If your sibling is open to talking to you, listen to his
opinions without trying to defend yourself or refute his point of
view. Ask for the same respect, too. When he tells you, "Your
room was much larger than mine," even though you are convinced
that they were both the same size, do not argue the point. Keep in
mind that in families each person views things from a different perspective and everyone's feelings are valid. Do not minimize the
issue either. As insignificant as it may seem to you, the extra foot or

two that he is complaining about may have pained him deeply over the years. Perhaps the belief that you had a larger room made him feel he was less loved. As we can see, the seemingly little things that brothers and sisters argue about often mask the larger issues. That is why they can become so highly charged, create constant friction, and even cause a rupture in the relationship.

Revealing past jealousies and anger can help them to dissipate. If each of you takes responsibility for your behaviors and apologizes, you are on the road to recovery. But this is only the beginning. You and your sibling(s) will need to work hard and process your feelings each time a new hurt occurs. You may find yourself saying the same things over and over again, but there is a payoff. This kind of open communication will help you relate more positively to each other and to your children. Remember, some of your anger and jealousy toward your sibling really has to do with anger at your parent. Once you redirect this anger in some way, even in your thoughts, you will feel more loving to your sibling.

Discuss your feelings with your parents, if you can. Some people are lucky enough to be able to go yet another step further. They discuss their feelings directly to one or both of their parents. Expressing your anger to a responsive parent that he or she showed favoritism toward your sibling can help you feel less upset. Your parent may even try to change his or her behavior.

It will be easier for your parent to listen to you and respond if you give him or her specific examples of what is troubling you, and if you present your issues without blame.

Resolution will be an ongoing process. As each new situation occurs in which you feel history is repeating itself, you will need to express your feelings again. You will also need to constantly set limits and structure situations carefully.

Discussing your emotions with your parents and your siblings can help free you of the hidden anger and guilt that you carry around, and allow you to be a better parent. If you get a good response, you will feel closer to them. When the anger melts away, loving feelings arise.

Find ways to make peace with the past. If your parents or siblings are not alive, or if you are estranged, you can still resolve some of your feelings on your own, and it is important that you do so. Allow yourself to experience all the feelings of love and anger that you have toward your sibling or parent. It is only when we face all the facets of our emotions about someone that we can come to a greater resolution.

If you are, in fact, estranged from a sibling or parent and you wish to try, you might reconsider reaching out to them again. Perhaps you can rebuild a relationship based upon the new insights and approaches you have gained from reading this book.

Through the analysis recommended above, you can become aware of how your feelings from your early birth order experiences are affecting your relationship with your child. Working through these emotions, on your own or with some professional assistance, will help you repair some of your earlier hurts and become a more effective parent.

Afterword

🐝 The topic of birth order is truly magnetic. Wherever I went as I was writing this book, everyone got involved. As I exercised with my physical therapist, he asked me questions about how to handle the rivalry between his two children. While my hairdresser was cutting my hair, she recounted her early childhood experiences as the only girl growing up with five brothers. It was clear to me that everyone had strong feelings about birth order, and in their thirst to understand themselves and their children better, they wanted to talk. Furthermore, I found that discussing birth order was helpful to people, whether it was in a random conversation at an airport, in a session with my patients or support group members, or during the formal interviews that I conducted for this project.

As I mentioned in the preface, I conducted many personal interviews while I was writing this book. In fact, I interviewed just about everyone I knew: parent support group members, friends, friends of friends, my family, and children of all ages. After I interviewed each one, I asked, "Do you think this discussion helped you?" And unanimously they agreed that it had.

The parents I spoke with about their children said that through the interviews, they had gained a deeper understanding of each of their children, a greater facility to talk to their children about their feelings, and many ideas about how to handle tough situations. Many parents also said that focusing on birth order issues had caused them to think more about their own early childhood experiences, and to become aware of what their parents had overlooked. As one secondborn mother put it, "Before we talked, I hadn't thought about the possibility of doing things differently." Now, this mother is able to give her children the kind of support that she wished she had had as a child.

The children I interviewed also seemed to benefit from the experience. But often what the children had to say placed me in a dilemma. The interviews were confidential, but the information they were giving me was really important for their parents to know about. I solved the problem either by suggesting that a child tell his or her parent about a particular feeling, or by asking if they would like me to tell.

The people who were most involved in this project and actually read the manuscript began to incorporate the ideas and make changes in their lives. My administrator, the secondborn of six, realized that she had always been a caretaker with her younger siblings and put their needs first. As she worked on the book, she began to concentrate more on her self and eventually asked her parents for help with buying a house.

My husband, who is a writer and has constantly read over my chapters, has begun to develop the characters in his stories keeping in mind the ideas in this book and feels that he can now portray them more accurately. I find it interesting, too, that everyone I know now walks around asking others, "What is your birth order?" in an effort to understand them—whether it's a social worker asking her clients for this crucial piece of background information or a woman asking her bossy new bridge partner on the Internet, "Are you a firstborn child?"

As for me, it would take another book to describe just how

much the process of writing this book and the material itself has helped me to understand myself, my relationships, and the people I work with. This experience has enriched my life forever.

It is my deepest wish that my book has done all of the above for you.

Getting
Professional
Help

🐝 Though birth order issues are common, everyday problems, they can be very hard to manage. After reading this book and trying out the suggestions, if you find that you need extra assistance, I recommend that you consider professional help. A therapist can help you to deal with a child who is very angry or oppositional; to diminish family battles; and improve your parent-child communication.

I have found that birth order issues are dealt with extremely well in family therapy. The beauty of working with these issues with the entire family present is that you have the whole cast of characters right in the room. As they interact, family members play out their typical patterns for the whole family to observe. Two siblings might fight over sitting in a particular chair, or a child who feels overlooked might engage in negative attention-seeking behavior. The family can then talk about what is going on, all together.

The therapist helps each member to explore how he or she feels and to understand his or her own behavior. With this greater awareness, family members can assume responsibility for their part in a situation and make more positive behavioral choices. At the same time, family members develop a deeper understanding of each other and a greater sensitivity to each other's emotional needs. With the therapist's guidance, the children and the parents learn to express their feelings in more constructive ways. These approaches are then internalized by the family members and become the way they resolve problems throughout life.

Joining a parent support group led by a professional is also a way to help your family. It can provide you with an ongoing, supportive framework to talk about any issues that are arousing your anxiety. As the parents talk together, they can clearly see that much of what they deal with in their relationships, whether it is a first-born child's anger after the birth of a second child or a younger child's jealousy at his older sibling's graduation, is common among parents and children, and this is very reassuring to them. Together, the group members search for ways to respond more positively to their children. The group leader is there to guide the parents, provide explanations for their children's behaviors, and offer the parents specific suggestions on how to manage situations with their children effectively.

Bibliography

General Psychology and Parenting Books

Alexander-Roberts, Colleen, and Mark T. Snyder, M.D. *Does My Child Need a Therapist?* Dallas, Texas: Taylor Publishing Company, 1997.

Adler, Alfred. *The Individual Psychology of Alfred Adler.* Edited by Heinz L. Ansbacher and Rowena R. Ansbacher. New York: Harper & Row, Publishers, 1956.

Dreikurs, Rudolf, M.D., with Vicki Soltz, R.N. *Children: The Challenge.* New York: Plume, 1964.

Eichenbaum, Luise, and Susie Orbach. *Between Women.* New York: Penguin Books, 1987.

Fraiberg, Selma. *The Magic Years.* New York: Charles Scribner's & Sons, 1959.

Freud, Sigmund *Freud, the Complete Introductory Lectures on Psychoanalysis.* Edited by James Strachey. New York: W. W. Norton & Company, 1966

Galinsky, Ellen, and Judy David. *The Preschool Years.* New York: Ballantine Books, 1988.

Ginott, Dr. Haim. *Between Parent and Child.* New York: Avon Books, 1956.

Grollman, Earl A. *Talking About Death.* Boston: Beacon Press, 1990.

Payne, Niravi B., M.S., and Brenda Lane Richardson. *The Whole Person Fertility Program.* New York: Three Rivers Press, 1997.

Samalin, Nancy, with Martha Moraghan Jablow. *Loving Your Child Is Not Enough.* New York: Penguin Books, 1987.

Turecki, Stanley, M.D., with Leslie Tonner. *The Difficult Child.* New York: Bantam Books, 1985.

Birth Order Books

Isaacson, Clifford, E. *How to Love Your Children.* Algona, Iowa: Upper Des Moines Counseling Center, Inc., 1992.

Leman, Dr. Kevin. *The Birth Order Book.* Grand Rapids, Michigan: Spire Books, 1985.

Richardson, Dr. Donald W., and Lois A. Richardson. *Birth Order and You.* New York: International Self-Counsel Press, Ltd., 1990.

Sulloway, Frank J. *Born to Rebel.* New York: Pantheon Books, 1996.

Toman, Walter, Ph.D. *Family Constellations.* New York: Springer Publishing Company, 1993.

Sibling Relationships

Ames, Louise Bates, with Carol Haber Chase. *He Hit Me First.* New York: Warner Books, 1982.

Arnston, Helene, S. *Brother and Sisters and Sisters and Brothers.* New York: E. P. Dutton, 1979.

Bank, Stephen P., and Michael D. Kahn. *The Sibling Bond.* New York: HarperCollins, 1997.

Dunn, Judy. *Sisters and Brothers.* Cambridge. Harvard University Press, 1985.

Faber, Adele, and Elaine Mazlish. *Siblings Without Rivalry.* New York: Avon Books, 1987.

Greer, Jane, with Edward Myers. *Adult Sibling Rivalry.* New York: Crown Publishers, 1992.

Hapworth, William and Mada, and Joan Rattner Heilman. *Mom Loved You Best.* New York: Penguin Books, 1993.

Klagsbrun, Francine. *Mixed Feelings.* New York: Bantam Books, 1992.

Reit, Seymour V. *Sibling Rivalry.* New York: Ballantine Books, 1985.

Samalin, Nancy, with Catherine Whitney. *Loving Each One Best.* New York: Bantam Books, 1990.

Weiss, Joan Solomon. *Your Second Child.* New York: Summit Books, 1981.

Only Children and Multiples

Clegg, Averil, and Anne Woolett. *Twins: From Conception to Five Years.* New York: Ballantine Books, 1983.

Friedrich, Elizabeth, and Cheryl Rowland. *The Parents' Guide to Raising Twins.* New York: St. Martin's Press, 1983.

Newman, Susan. *Parenting an Only Child.* New York: Doubleday, 1990.
Rothbard, Betty, and Ronald M. Caplan. *Multiple Blessings.* New York: Hearst Books, 1994.
Sefford, Darrell. *The Only Child.* New York: Harper & Row: 1989.

Gender-Related Issues

Caron, Ann F. *Strong Mothers, Strong Sons.* New York: HarperPerennial, 1994.
Eagle, Dr. Carol J., and Carol Colman. *All That She Can Be.* New York: Fireside, 1993.
Gadeberg, Jeanette. *Raising Strong Daughters.* Minneapolis, Minn.: Fairview Press, 1995.
Gurion, Michael. *The Wonder of Boys.* New York: G. P. Putnam's Sons, 1997.
Laskin, David, and Kathleen O'Neil. *The Little Girl Book.* New York: Ballantine Books, 1992.
Mackoff, Dr. Barbara. *Growing Up a Girl.* New York: Bantam Doubleday Dell Publishing Group, 1996.
Miedzian, Myriam. *Boys Will Be Boys.* New York: Anchor Books, 1991.
Pipher, Mary, Ph.D. *Reviving Ophelia.* New York: Ballantine Books, 1994.

Children's Books

Amos, Janine. *Jealous.* New York: Steck-Vaughn Company, 1991.
Blume, Judy. *The One in the Middle Is the Green Kangaroo.* New York: A Picture Yearling Book, 1981.
Cole, Joanna. *The New Baby at Your House.* New York: Morrow Junior Books, 1985.
Corey, Dorothy. *Will There Be a Lap for Me?* Morton Grove, Illinois: Albert Whitman & Company, 1992.
Hazen, Barbara Shook. *If It Weren't for Benjamin.* New York: Human Sciences Press, 1979.
Horowitz, Ruth. *Mommy's Lap.* New York: Lothrop, Lee & Shepard Books, 1993.
Hurwitz, Johanna. *Elisa in the Middle.* New York: Morrow Junior Books, 1995.
Hutchins, Pat. *Titch.* New York: First Aladdin Books, 1993.
Margolis, Richard. *Secrets of a Small Brother.* New York: Macmillan Publishing Co., 1984.
Rogers, Fred. *The New Baby.* New York: G. P. Putnam's Sons, 1985.
Scott, Elaine. *Twins.* New York: Atheneum Books for Young Readers, 1998.
Senisi, Ellen B. *Brothers & Sisters.* New York: Scholastic, 1993.

Research Articles and Studies

Bouchard, Thomas J., Jr. "Whenever the Twain Shall Meet." *The Sciences* (September/October 1997).

Goode, Erica E. "The Secret World of Siblings," *U.S. News and World Report,* 116 (January 10, 1994): 44.

Griffone, Robert J., and Leonard Biandri. "Effects of Ordinal Position on Academic Self-Concept." *Psychological Reports* 55 (1984): 263–268.

Hagekull, Benit, and Gunilla Bohlin. "Prevalence of Problematic Behavior in Four-Year-Olds." *Scandinavian Journal of Psychology* 33 (1992): 359–369.

Harris, M.J., K. John, and R. Sharp. "The Effects of a Mother's Second Pregnancy on the Firstborn Child." *Australia and New Zealand Journal of Obstetrics and Gynaecology* 29, no. 3(2) (1989): 319.

Ilechukwu, Sunny T.C., M.B., "Sibling Rivalry as an Important Factor in Under-achievement: A Cross-Cultural Contribution." *Psychiatric Journal of the University of Ottawa* 13, no. 3 (1988).

Jacobs, Blanche A., and Howard A. Moss. "Birth Order and Sex of a Sibling as Determinants of Mother-Infant Interaction." National Institute of Mental Health., *Child Development* (1976).

Leung, Alexander K.D., M.B.B.S.R.C.P.C., F.A.A.P., F.R.S.H., and William Lane Robson, M.D., "Sibling Rivalry," *Clinical Pediatrics* 30, no. 5.

Mander, Gertrude. "Some Thoughts on Sibling Rivalry and Competitiveness." *British Journal of Psychotherapy* (1991).

Neubauer, Peter B., M.D. "The Importance of the Sibling Experience." *The Psychoanalytic Study of the Child,* 89 (1983): 325–329.

Stanton, Feehan M., W. McGee, and R. Silva, P.A. "A Longitudinal Study of Birth Order, Help Seeking and Psychopathology." *British Journal of Clinical Psychology* 33 (1994): 143–150.

Wright, Lawrence. "Double Mystery." *The New Yorker* (August 7, 1995).

Young, Paul C., M.D., Kathleen Boyle, R.N., M.S., and Richard B. Colletti, "Maternal Reaction to the Birth of a Second Child: Another Side of Sibling Rivalry." *Child Psychiatry and Human Development* 14, no. 1 (fall–1998).

Index

About the Author

MERI WALLACE, M.S.W., C.S.W., a therapist specializing in the treatment of children and families, is the founder of the Heights Center for Adult and Child Development in Brooklyn Heights, New York. She conducts parent support groups and workshops and is a consultant to nursery schools. Ms. Wallace is the author of *Keys to Parenting Your Four Year Old* and is a columnist for *Sesame Street Parents* magazine. She is also a contributor to several other parenting magazines.